It's All In The Journey

It's All In The Journey

AN EXERCISE IN FAITH

Lesa Hunt

Complete Restoration Publishing

This work is dedicated to all of those that have suffered from childhood abuse. To all those who have suffered abuse as an adult who have gone through the trauma of that abuse. Know that you are special and you are important your voice needs to be heard and you are going to make it you are overcomers. To my darling children I know it's been a long road, but we made it thank you for being there and encouraging me when I wanted to give up. This one is for you!!

It's All in the Journey

Dear Overcomer Through Faith,

Through the guidance and love of the Holy Spirit, you have made an exceptional step. In choosing to let God help you transcend from being a survivor of the Abuse in your past to being an overcome of the entire experience. With the help and guidance of Jesus Christ and the comfort of the Holy Ghost, it is my prayer and sincere hope that something contained within this book will help you heal. With all the hurt you have gone through and the pain you have been hiding for so long, I know you are wondering how you survive. I am here to tell you; surviving is what you already do. Overcoming is where you want and need to be. I must warn you; this is a journey worth taking; it is long, and it will get hard, but I encourage you to take each day one step at a time and keep God close. You will make it through, remember you are not alone; you do not have to tackle this by yourself; others have been where you are; I have walked this path and know first-hand how lonely, tiring, frustrating, and anxious this journey is. Remember, the reward of peace of mind, a more meaningful relationship with the Father, and genuinely connecting with those around you are vital to a healthy existence. Stay focused, and don't doubt this process. I am here with you and for you as you face this challenge head-on. This is not just my story; this is my life, and my pleasure to share these strategies and hope with you; keep in mind, just as it was all in the journey with Jesus for me, it will be for you too.

May God continue to prosper you and help you stay grounded in Him. With Much prayer and love, we welcome you to the first step in the renewing of your spirit.

Faithfully Yours,
Apostle Lesa Hunt

Overcomers

For God hath not given us the spirit of fear, but of power and of love and of a sound mind. 1 Timothy 1:7

Always Remember:

For I am persuaded that neither death nor life nor angels nor principalities nor powers nor things present nor things to come, nor height nor depth nor any other creature shall be able to separate us from the love of God, which is in Christ Jesus our Lord.

Romans 8:38, 39

The mountains and the streams seem to run together in a pattern as old as time. I have watched for so many years. My days seem longer now than they were when I was young. I wonder if the things I am experiencing currently are the things that I should be or if there is something else out there for me. I have asked myself repeatedly, did I make the right decision? However, now my only question is whether I can fulfill the obligation to do a more excellent work. The wind in the middle of my heart seems to whisper to me to go further, and my body seems to respond. I am sitting here in the middle of a beautiful moment in my life; this is when I have finally realized that GOD is the only reason I could be born, for there is something that HE has for me to do. To do it, I must be ready to accept all aspects of HIS calling.

This book is not about how to rid yourself of all the bad things in your life. This book is about telling others out there, like me, who have suffered hardships and pain that GOD can and will supply all your needs in this life if you just let HIM do it for you.

From the Heart of the Author.

First, let me tell you a bit about myself. I know you may ask why you would write about abuse and how to move beyond it? Or who is she to write about this? Or has she ever been through what I have? I want help; I want to trust that this will work, but why this book? I don't need another self-help, but no use, line of a mess that people say helped them, but they are still stuck in the same mindset. Something that will last is what I need. Can she really help me, and if so, does she know how I am feeling right now? I am here to tell you this book can help you on your journey. However, it is not a fix all you will have to be open, and you will have to work at overcoming the abuse. You must be a willing participant in this process the only way for you to move though this is that you apply yourself to the process without your, complete engagement there can be no complete change.

Let me settle your mind and possibly answer some of your questions. The following is some of my testimony to let you know God didn't just say to me to write a book. God said to me, tell your story so that others may be healed just as I healed you. I want you to understand I have been through a lot, and I did not want to be too graphic however there are parts of my story that my trigger you. If you are not ready to go it alone, please find someone whom you trust or with similar life experiences as you have and begin this journey together. I was born in a small town in the south of the United States. My mother, who was alone, separated from my dad. Years later, I was told that she did what she thought was the best for me for many reasons, some of which I struggled for years to understand. While others I still sometimes question. After 11 months, my dad won custody of my brother and me in an unfair, totally biased courtroom according to my mother's account of the events. My father always told me differently. His version was that my mother, walking into a courtroom with me, placed me on the bench next to him and walked away. Knowing my mother as I now do, I suspect the truth lies somewhere in the middle of both their accounts of the event.

By my mother's recollection, my father used the power of one handshake because he was, and my family still is part of what some consider a prestigious organization that carried at the time the ability to have anything you want to be delivered to you And what my dad wanted involved making my mom suffer for leaving him, according to her. I am still not sure of my father's motivation other than that he has always stated that my mother was crazy, and I must admit after spending all the years I did with my mother I can understand his saying that even though she is not crazy, my mother operates in a perpetual state of complete and total psychological manipulation and torment of those around her. However, my father was no victim in the story of my life either, at least not from my point of view.

My father was the son of one of the most influential and high-ranking members of his house within this organization, affording him certain rights and privileges at his leisure. By taking her children, my father achieved one mission, and that was to strike a blow to my mother from which she could never recover. Because she left him the manner she did after years of his cheating and mutual physical abuse between the two, he accomplished that. For my mother, losing her two-and-a-half-year-old son and her 11-month-old daughter was devastating. The impact added to what had already been many years of abuse and neglect, hurt and molestation that already had my mother's mind and spirit in a horrible place. My mother was broken and lost for many years, and the demons she battled overtook her many times. Shortly after the court battle was won, was the first recorded incident of abuse perpetrated on me according to my mother's recollection and what is known in medical records. My first birthday was a week away. I was forcibly penetrated by wooden objects and yes; I was raped for the first time at that time as well. Was I given back to my mother then? No, and it is my opinion since I suffered terrible acts of abuse and molestation it seemed to me for years that when you have the power to do what you want because of who you are associated with and your involvement in an elitist organization, they look over things like that.

The man I knew as my father was essentially a womanizer who used his power and influence as the leader of his congregation to exact favors from all kinds of people. His ability to use his influence and manipulate others into doing what he wanted for his own pleasure and personal gain was something that I noticed early in life. He married several women over the years all of whom I was expected to call mom, and I did because it was just easier that way and because I knew that if I didn't, I would end up being beaten almost to death for disrespecting them. I watched him use, abuse, and mistreat them over and over. One of his wives I felt sorry for because of her passive nature. She was a quiet, reserved woman who laughed at everything he did. She was in love; you could tell she just wanted to please him. She wanted to do whatever he asked her of her. I was seven or eight years old when he married her, and they would stay married until after the birth of my firstborn son. I would later in my life at the tender age of Eleven witness him beating and stomping on her until she miscarried laying on the living room floor. She tried to please him, but nothing she did was ever good enough. He wouldn't let her call him pet names; she had to call him by his title Elder.

That made no sense to me, not only that the fact that she did it made no sense to me either. She was so loyal to him and genuinely devoted, yet the women he slept with at every church he pastored would treat her like crap, and he let them. She would work hard all day and come home to meet his crazy demands. She never got a moment's peace, and the few times when she was happy, he would beat or verbally abuse her until she wasn't. I learned from their relationship that I never wanted to be that way. When I was older and still not out of high school, I ended up with someone like that who beat me and mistreated me, and I thought for a long time that I deserved to be treated that way.

When I was young, the most challenging thing for me was living with my grandmother, or shall I say, the woman I thought was my grandmother. It turns out she was technically more my great-grandmother. To give you further insight, I am the offspring of a mother who married into the same family as her aunt and the man I knew as my dad was himself a child born from the incestuous relationship between a father and his daughter. Can you keep up? Or even understand what that means? Don't worry; it took years for me to figure out essentially my mother was not only my mother by birth but my aunt by marriage because she married into the same family as her aunt, who was my grandmother's sister on my mother's side. My dad was my dad, and my uncle and cousin twice removed. My biological father I would later find out was in fact one of my uncles on my father's side whom he called his brother but was technically his brother and his uncle because he was the product of my grandfather's sexually incestuous relationship with one of his daughters.

I desperately wanted a mother during my childhood; I needed someone who would love me through it all and protect me. My grandmother was too old and mean, sometimes downright cruel. Sometimes she didn't want to be bothered or even acknowledge that I was alive. My brother and I were her little workers, more like live-in slaves was how it felt. She would send us to the field early in the morning before dawn, and sometimes we would work until well into the heat of the day and into the early evening hours, depending on what was needed on the farm.

We would be out there in the heat with no water, no protection from the elements; our only task was to harvest peas, beans, corn, tomatoes, okra, squash, peanuts, tobacco, or whatever was growing. I felt like a workhorse instead of a child. In my world, children were seen and not heard. I know that being raised the way at the time was hard, but now I am grateful for the lessons that hard work and perseverance that it taught me. There were harsh consequences for the smallest of things. It was more difficult for me because I never got a moment's peace. I had so much come at me all the time. That I had to stay twenty paces ahead of my sibling, both biological and step-siblings, always. I know it is said that what doesn't kill you will strengthen you. But to be beaten until you bleed or starved or being prohibited from getting a simple a drink of water without permission after working the fields in the heat all day. In combination with repeated molestation and rape from various male and female members of my family, these things are hard. And I know every child must endure some things growing up that they may not like, however in my opinion no child should have to endure what I did.

I remember thinking that my grandmother was so mean. I never took into consideration that she was overwhelmed. I never thought that she had it hard, too; after all, she was married to a man at the tender age of 13, much older than her. Twice her age, to be exact, she was treated like a piece of property. Her only function is to cook, clean, work the farm, have babies, and serve him in every way. In my mind to this day, it is a long time (they were married for over 55 years) to be someone's property. Giving birth to over 17 children, some of them dying very early in their lives, and she was never given the chance to grieve properly. She learned early to keep going and hide her emotions and feelings within. As I got older after he died, I would see it sometimes, the pain and sorrow in her eyes. By the time my brother and I came along, there were seven of her children remaining of my uncles and aunts, all of which I do not have a relationship with to this day. This was not necessarily by force, but a conscious choice on my part. I could not face them as a child after I left home at 14 and chose not to entertain them as an adult.

So, it must have been hard for her to open her home in her old age to two small children because my dad wanted to be selfish and take us from our mother, and rather than be saddled with raising us give us to her to raise. For that reason, at first, I didn't know who my dad was although I saw him every day, but I didn't make the connection that he was my dad, and ever since I was little, I didn't like the man. I don't recall staying with my dad that often, but one of the few times I did, my older stepbrother sodomized me. I was about six years old; he was not the first, and I am sorry to say not the last. Over the 14 years I lived with these people, I was raped, sodomized, burned, beaten, molested, sold for sex, and used in witchcraft rituals too many times to count.

One of the earliest memories I have is of one of my abusers raping me at three. It lasted only a few fleeting moments, but the act itself would stay with me for years to come. I can still remember the sights, sounds, smells, emotions and feelings of that day. Only now the pain of the moment does not send me into a tailspin as it used to. When he was done, he pushed me away from him like I was nasty or a piece of filthy rag. I wrapped my arms around myself and cried when I looked up; my older stepsister was watching. She said nothing, and she never tried to stop him. I had no one to protect me; I felt utterly isolated and alone. From that moment on, I always had a problem with my older stepsister. I recall she would make all the other kids in the house play games involving sexual things. Usually, things like you must do what I say do or Simon says only the adult version. Inevitably, someone would end up in bed with me. We would then be told to perform certain acts on each other and then for the next two or three months, every time she wanted me to do something that I didn't want to do, if I refused, she would say that she was going to tell what I had done. I knew enough about sex to see that it was wrong, but I wasn't sure why she would make us do it and then threaten to tell on us for doing it. I also knew the consequences that would come from her telling, and the thought of being tied to something and beaten within an inch of my life was not something I wanted either. Fear kept me in line, fear and intimidation coupled with manipulation.

This was a regular part of my life as a child. Some man or woman or cousin or uncle or friend of my brothers from up the road or someone my brother has promised me to, was always doing inappropriate things to me. Life was supposed to be like this is what I thought for a long time. I remember not wanting to come home from school because I was scared; I felt like I would be jumped on any second. I had friends at school, people I could laugh with and not be afraid school was a place I could get away from my life for a little while. The ride home on the bus was always the hardest. The closer we got to the house, the worse I would feel. People always said that I looked sad and scared most of the time, and most of the time, I was. I endured sadistic treatment from my brother almost daily. If he wasn't throwing something at me, he dropped things on me. When I was seven, he climbed a tree and dropped a large brick on my head. I still suffer from headaches and cluster migraines sometimes from that one. But there was also sexual abuse with him too.

For a long time, the memories bothered me, especially the things my brother did to me. When he would abuse me sexually, it was as if he wanted it to hurt; he was always rough. If I weren't crying, he would hit me or use objects instead just to see me cry. He would hit me for no reason and once even chopped me in the head with a garden hoe. It was as if my brother needed me to be in pain or hurt for his day to be better. I wouldn't say he liked it, but when my brother was in a bad mood; it was me; he tormented. He would seek me out and torment or torture me. If I were playing alone, he would find me and knock me down and sexually abuse me. He would tie me up sometimes and beat me with extension cords or branches from trees around the property. On one occasion, I recall him climbing a tree with a rope. He convinced me to climb up with him; he knew I was afraid of heights so he said that he would hold my hand. He promised he would not let go. I didn't think anything of it when I was almost up on the limb; he threw the rope around my neck and let my hand go. For what felt like an eternity, I hung by my neck. I felt myself passing out. The laughter I heard was from him. I knew I was going to die that day. I would have if it were not for the grace of God. The rope broke. To cover the rope marks on my neck, I had to go to school for a few weeks in turtleneck shirts. What did I do to deserve what I went through?

That was the hardest thing for me growing up, not knowing when the next time someone was going to rape, beat, molest, or hurt me in some other way. The not knowing when I was going to get a beating to the point of bleeding from my grandmother or get cursed at by my dad or worse, getting beat and cursed at by someone else. Still, there were some good times in my childhood as well. One of them is the week that I gave my life to Christ.

I was saved when I was eleven years old. I was sitting out in my grandmother's yard singing from the Baptist hymnbook. I used to love to sing; it was the one thing that made me happy as a child. While singing, his eye is on the sparrow. Under that tree, the word of the Lord came to me and said, you will preach my word. I was both afraid and excited simultaneously; however, where I grew up and the family I grew up in, women could not preach or become ministers. They were discouraged whenever they wanted to pursue a life in the ministry. I remember my grandfather saying that gal has a calling on her life, but there ain't nothing she can do about it. My dad said that I differed from the other children that I was just funny acting. I wouldn't play with my brother and cousin, and I was usually off by myself with a hymnbook singing or what they called play preaching. It was the one peace in my life,

I loved singing and talking to God, even as a child, with that innocence we all had when we were young. I would sing for hours and play like I was preaching to the cats and dogs or even to the birds' anything that I could use as an audience. My brother and cousin would ask me if I was crazy or stupid when they weren't hitting me or molesting me, tying me down, throwing bugs on me, or chasing me with sticks.

When we were in church, I remember the following Sunday when dad said, does anyone desire to be saved and baptized? I walked to the church's front. I didn't mean to move I didn't want to give my daddy my hand, the man who would curse at me one minute, beat me another say he loved me the next, then touch me in places that he shouldn't after that, but it wasn't him I was giving my hand to that Sunday it was God. The room felt suddenly void of air. I thought I was going to pass out. The little wooden church seemed so big at that moment then my feet moved, and I felt myself going forward each step I took I felt lighter and lighter tears streamed down my face, and I couldn't see in front of me by the time I got to my dad my hands were shaking. I noticed a tear in his eye; he stood in front of me, tall and looking afraid at that moment and speechless for the first time in my life. Nothing could have ruined that moment for me; it was at that moment I knew God had something he wanted me to do, and I was going to do it no matter what. If I had known, then that Satan would attack me more than he already had. I don't know what I would have done.

The day I was baptized, I was in a euphoria state, and I felt as if my life finally had a purpose, a meaning. I was not sure what that meaning was, but I knew God would use me for more than just singing gospel music. I knew that there was a reason all the things that had happened to me did not make me weaker, but stronger. There was a reason I was alive. however, what I did not know then was that if I weren't careful, Satan would try to take away all that GOD had placed in me.

Day in and day out, housework, school, yard work, more work, and all the while, someone was hitting me, molesting, or raping me, or starving me, or telling me I would never amount to anything. Or telling me I was crazy just like my mother or saying things like you are so useless. That is why your mother didn't want you. Going to church with my dad on Sunday morning when we started going with him was the worst for me because he would spend the entire car ride saying the cruelest things. I was a nasty little (b....). I was told that I would be nothing more than a whore; I was useless; I was nothing. I couldn't do anything right. Everything that I did was (f.. ed) up. I was a stupid little (S.O. B), a crazy (muther......) I was a piece of (s...). I would sit there and cry.

I was usually an emotional wreck by the time I got to church. His wife was so afraid that she would not stand up to him and tell him he was wrong, so she was no help. I remember thinking that I must be the worst kid in the world. My mother didn't want me. I used to look at myself in the mirror and say, look at you, no one wants you, no one loves you. Your mother walked off and left you with these people who hate you. Your dad doesn't know about your birthday; he doesn't know how old you are. He doesn't care about you; he only loves his son; you mean nothing to anyone in this family. You are only a sex object. No man will ever want you except for having sex with you. That feeling would carry on with me into much of my adult life. I would often feel like I was never good enough, or that I would never amount to anything, or that I was ugly, and that no man would ever want to love me.

These things take a toll on the body, mind, and spirit, and after a while, I believed I was nothing and that I would be nothing and that I would never amount to anything. Those feelings also translated into my relationship with my biological mother. When we first met each other, I felt so rejected that it was hard to get past it. But now that I am older and wiser, I know I am more than a conquer, and I am something I am unique in the eyesight of God, and I am special to myself, and that is all that matters.

At 11, I found myself pregnant; that was one of the worst days. I remember being taken to the doctor by my aunt and my grandmother. This was the first time I was to have a complete female exam, and I was timid. The doctor was a man, and I was uncomfortable around men as it was, and now this man was going to be looking at parts of my body that I didn't voluntarily show anyone. I was not in the room alone. My grandmother and aunt were both in the room watching everything he did. I felt like I was on display; I wanted to die. I didn't want anyone looking at me like that; I was not comfortable looking at my body, so I was out of my element, having three people watching me.

When the exam was finished, the doctor announced that I was three months pregnant. Here I was, going into the eighth grade. Pregnant, I felt alone. I was afraid I wanted to die. I knew nothing about having a baby. My dad nor my grandmother never really talked to me about sex. All that I knew about sex was what I learned from the library at school after reading several books on reproduction.

After sexual education in school, I knew I was pregnant by the symptoms, but I didn't want to believe it, and I certainly didn't want it, and the most challenging part was, I did not know who the father of my baby was. I remember thinking why my grandmother kept saying, tell me who the father is? Why would she want me to tell her who the father was when she knew I went nowhere but to school and home? If she knew my brother was having sex with me, why didn't she stop it? At that moment, I realized they knew what was going on, and they did nothing to help me for the past 11 years of my life. They knew I was getting raped by my brother and others, and they did not stop it. They knew, and they did not help me. She said she knew I was letting him touch me. I knew you were opening your legs to him; I knew he shouldn't be around you. You had better tell me, and I mean you tell me now those words still ring in my ears sometimes. Here I am, 11 and pregnant, scared and alone, not knowing what to do next, and all she could think about was how embarrassed she was of me and my nasty little (a..) and my evil little brother. I remember being so angry I yelled at her, saying, you only want me to tell you it is my brother so that I won't say that there is a chance that this baby may belong to your son as well. What they didn't know was I had been taken one day about three months prior by force, tied up, blindfolded, and taken somewhere away from school. When I arrived at the location, I was tied to something hard. The room smelled old and stale. My heart raced I knew I was in trouble. I heard someone describing that they had a young one here she isn't pure but by experience she is well worth it. At that point, I knew they were talking about me. There were several men who had intercourse with me that day. How could this happen to me? I have since learned the events from that day were extruded and planned by members of my family. I was essentially sold off for sex that day.

She was furious. She threatened to beat me. My emotions we so on edge that I didn't care; I was devastated; I spent the next few weeks crying uncontrollably. I turned 12 the next month, and in March of the following year, I gave birth to a baby boy. It was the hardest thing that I had to do. Labor was hard on me. I was in pain for two days. I didn't say anything to my grandmother; I just kept going by that time. No one was going to help me.

I was in a school for pregnant girls, so I woke up nauseous and feeling like I was going to die on the third day. I was tired and in pain. I was having contractions but not in a pattern, so I thought it was false labor. Besides, the baby wasn't due for another three weeks. I got myself ready for school. I knew if I could get there, I could talk to the nurse coming in that day to get some help. I walked to the bus stop, got on the bus, and lay down the entire ride to school. The pain kept coming; I don't remember being scared; I remember thinking that I was glad that it would be over. When I got to school, I went in and waited until the nurse got there. When she did, I remember saying that we needed to talk. She checked, and I was indeed in labor on the drive to the hospital; one teacher drove me. I was calm, too calm. When I got there, my dad's wife met us there; someone brought my grandmother. I didn't want any of them there; I wanted my mother. I didn't want to be in that situation.

I just wanted my mother. As the pains got worse, I wanted her more. I felt utterly alone and scared, even though the room was full of people. I wanted desperately for the pain to end, and I wanted to be a kid again. I knew that my childhood was over, but then again, I never really acted like a child, so I was unsure how being a mother would be any different. I wasn't sure I could be an exemplary mother; I knew I didn't want to be a mother. I know that is hard to say, but at 12 and sexually molested and raped all your life, who wants to be a mother that way?

I didn't know who his dad was. I didn't know how to explain how he came to be when the time came; no loving husband was holding my hand as we brought a new and innocent life into this world. There was no happy, supportive family, just the people who knew what was happening in my home, the nightmare that I faced and did nothing to stop it so that it now was clear to the world that something was going on. Still, that was explained away. The story was told that I was a wayward preacher's daughter, that I was rebelling against my dad, and that I had gone out and gotten pregnant by the first little boy that showed me some attention. I felt trapped by this life and this existence that grieved me so much.

I tried to be an exemplary mother, but I didn't know how to be. I would look at my son and think with dread about when he got older and when he would ask questions about his dad. I was depressed to where I started lashing out. I became outraged. I was angry with the people who hurt me, angry with those who stood by and knew what

I was going through and did nothing. I was mad at my dad and all his wives, furious that it appeared everyone was pleased telling the story of how I shamed the family and how I was a girl that slept around.

These people never even saw me show an interest in boys, so I was hurt. I began a relationship with one girl who went to school with me; yes, I said she was one of the first people to show me affection. For that reason, I was caught up in a lifestyle that I knew nothing about, but I was happy we talked every day, and she even came to visit me at my grandmother's home once or twice, but that stopped when my dad and other family found out about her.

I was even more isolated and hurt after our relationship ended. My dad started taking me to therapy, and the doctor prescribed antidepressants. I soon found that I could self-medicate to cope. So, I would only take my pills when someone said something to anger me or felt like I didn't want to be bothered. By the time I was 14, I began a relationship with one of the first men that I had dated on my own. I was going through a struggle to get rid of the pain of the life that I lived. I fell for a big-time drug dealer because he had the drugs that I wanted. I remember starting small, and then I used more and more; soon, I was up to a 200-dollar day habit. Still, it didn't affect me because of who I was with while high.

I allowed him to do things to me, and I remember thinking that I deserved it because I was worthless anyway. He beat me daily; he was cold and cruel. I realized I learned this behavior from watching my dad and how he treated every wife. I had fallen into that same thing that I didn't want to fall into; I was a whore to this man. When he didn't want to have sex with me, he would get me high and sell me to his friends. He would tell me I had to do this for him if I loved him. Our relationship ended when he beat me so badly one day that I ended up in the hospital. I didn't even know my name when I came out of the hospital; I learned he was dead, beaten down in the street, and then shot; that is the nature of the life of a drug dealer. I was 14 when I left home for good. My grandmother had, without my permission, sent my son to live with an aunt in another city. When I went to get him back, they would not let me have him. I was alone and angry with the life I lived. I felt defeated.

Soon I found someone that I was what I thought at the time I was in love with, but over the next few months, I started letting my grades slip. I dropped out and started drinking and smoking and doing drugs every day; I was considered an alcoholic when I was close to my 16th birthday. I spiraled into a world of drugs and depression, destructive behavior being sexually promiscuous. I allowed anything to be done to me just to be with someone. I wanted desperately to feel loved and not feel alone and afraid anymore, but I felt more and more isolated and frustrated I hid things from the man I was with while he worked during the day. I would do cocaine and drink. I would have sex with random men. I developed an eating disorder. I would binge all day. Then I would take laxatives or purge. I got pregnant twice while with him and had all those pregnancies' end in miscarriages.

I was lost, and in despair, I for a while forgot about being saved; that part of my life seemed so far away, and even though I would still sing at church functions, sometimes I felt lost, and without purpose, I was angry with God for allowing all that happened to me. I was mad at myself for not being able to stop what happened. At the age is 16, I tried for the first time to commit suicide. It did not work; I wanted to die. I couldn't live the way I was living anymore. I felt unwanted and unloved; I needed guidance, and everywhere I turned, I found none.

I was sinking and could not recover, so I turned to a bottle of pills one night, which I washed down with a glass of water mixed with bleach. But God had other plans; I lived and spent time in a mental facility for the next few months. It was during that time I was reintroduced to my mother, three months later; it was as if she had come to my rescue. She quit her job and came to stay with me. I was out of the hospital, and I thought that all was going to be well, but it was not we had a hard time adjusting to each other she wanted to be a mother to me, and I was in the mode of feeling as if I was an adult and did not need to be raised over.

Unfortunately, there was also abuse with her as well. Emotional, physical, and even sexual as well. We fought a lot and argued. I didn't realize it, but I was angry at her for a long time. I was mad that she was not there and did not help me. I was mad that when she came into my life; she was just as cruel, unforgiving, and heartless as my father's family. I would lash out, and so would she. Our relationship became physically violent at one point. I never hit my mother when I was younger, but she hit me. I did not know all that she was facing. I know she was raped and abused as a child; she was beaten severely by her mother, so she tried to cope with her issues when she came to rescue me.

Still, now that I am older and wiser, I can see things more clearly, and I am grateful that God has been here to guide and direct me through it all. I lived with my mother for over twenty years, and through it all, we fought. In the beginning, it was me fighting to be heard, fighting for her understanding of the pain I was in. I understood that she, too, was broken, but I could not understand why she still seemed stuck in the same spot.

I grew spiritually and matured in Christ, but my mother was different. She would walk around saying that she was a woman of God but living the opposite. As I sought God for direction, strength, and understanding for the things that I endured. She seemed to become stagnant. She was cold, calculated a force that seemed impenetrable, unyielding, void of any feeling other than hatred and self-loathing. When God called me into ministry officially at twenty-five, she grew resentful. God would minister through me to help others who needed guidance and direction; she would spend days and countless hours telling me I was evil, saying that if people knew who I was, they would not listen to me.

Even to the point of threatening to sue me if I published this book, saying that if I spoke negatively about her, she would make sure that I paid for it. Still, I pursued God with all that I had and still do. He is my foundation, and through Him, I have healed and endeavor to make sure that I help others make it through the things that keep them bound. These were some memories I faced after I married my first husband and tried to start a family. I have since understood that all I went through was tied to a generational curse. It was a way that the enemy got into my bloodline and caused generation after generation to perpetuate the same cycle.

It was a constant struggle when I first got to a place of deliverance to remove the hurtful thing and the pain and shame of abuse. I have spent countless hours on my knees in prayer, asking God for direction and instruction. When man failed me asking for peace and the memories not to drown me, and he has answered me, I turned to God. Understanding and accepting that these things happened to me and knowing I survived, was only because of my relationship no matter how tenuous with God. It took me a while to realize what truly happened in my life was not God's fault. It was something that my family members did.

Through all of that, I have learned to believe it or not, love them and pray for them as I pray for others in this life. I understand what you have just read may be a little graphic, but I said these things for a reason. I want you to know that you are not alone and that I have been through some of the same struggles as you, but if I could make it and prosper, you can.

The changes you will face while reading this book will affirm that GOD will never leave you or forsake you. He will never turn away from you in your time of need. I know it seems complicated because you feel you are the only one, but know that you are not alone; you are an overcomer. I know what it takes and how much effort it consumes to fight the memories alone. God does not want you to fight them alone. He wants you to understand that He will fight your battles if you just give them over to him. With that thought in mind, and now knowing the struggle that I, the author of this book, have faced, ask yourself, are you ready to live? Are you prepared to trust God when you can't trace Him? Even if you do not have a relationship with God, are you willing and ready to have a relationship with Him? I'm not talking about being tied to a religion or dogma of belief but to have an authentic relationship, where you learn to cast all your care on Him because He cares for you. You have taken the first step; you bought this book, or someone has given it to you, and you read this far. That is because a part of you yearns for freedom from the hurt and pain that abuse left you holding.

Complete the Journey with The Father, and with me, let Him through my journey show you just how much you mean to Him and what He will do to get you safely through your storm. Take the Journey. I know it is going to be worth it for you in the end. You will make it, and you are an overcomer!

FOOD FOR THOUGHT AND REFLECTION.
Questions:

1. *Take this time to write out your testimony, write out some of the abuse you suffered, write how you feel about the abuse right now.*
2. *Ask yourself, are you ready to end the cycle of pain and hurt you are or have experienced because of the abuse?*
3. *How do you feel about God? Are you angry at Him or have you ever been introduced to Him?.*

What exactly are we facing?

First, we need to know exactly what we are dealing with. There is a natural war between good and evil, and yes, there is a heaven and a hell. God and the devil are real, and we as human beings have the free will to choose right or wrong. Some actual demons in this world cause us to be hurt and oppressed. They inhabit those who are open and do not adequately understand the spiritual world.

You must understand that you are not fighting against flesh and blood. The bible says, "For though we walk in the flesh we do not war after the flesh for the weapons of out warfare are not carnal but are mighty through God to the pulling down of strongholds casting down imaginations and every high thing that exalted itself against the knowledge of God and bringeth into captivity every thought to the obedience of Christ and having in a readiness to revenge all disobedience when your obedience is fulfilled," 2 Corinthians 10:3-6 KJV.

What am I getting at? Simply, this abuse is not of God. It is not something that God intended for man to experience. Still, man's wickedness allows the enemy to control some thoughts of those who abuse, setting the victim's stage to deal with all kinds of demonic oppression and sometimes possession. So, ask yourself, are you sure you are ready to start this process? Are you prepared to deal with some complicated issues? Ensure that you are prepared to deal with the deep places that exploring abuse will inevitably bring up.

While I am not a secular counselor, I am a Spiritual Counselor. Yes, I have gone to school and been trained, but that is not where this book is coming from. This book has information learned while I was training and learning about some of my own issues. Yes, I am an Apostle and a leader and have the skills to counsel, but that is not where this book is coming from. I want you to understand me clearly.

This book has been birthed from all my experience, from my mother's experience and years of talking with countless other women who have been through some form of abuse or the other. It contains some clinical reference for a better understanding of some things that you may be facing. It is not a replacement for actual therapy if you feel you need it. This book is filled with information and a practical teaching on how I could endure and overcome the abuse. This is a personal experience that I wanted to share with you, hoping something that I learned in the process would help you understand your own journey. This has been a journey that I was set on from the foundation of the world. It is what I was put here to do. It is for the healing of a nation of others who, like me, have gone through the devastation of abuse, rape, torture, and torment. I would not be here if it had not been for the father keeping me.

"Little children (believers, dear ones), you are of God, and you belong to Him and have [already] overcome them [the agents of the antichrist]; because He who is in you is greater than he (Satan) who is in the world [of sinful mankind].1 John 4:4 Amplified Bible.

I have the pleasure of expressing real gut emotions and feelings with this subject. Everything in this book is written to tell you of my journey and how the love of the savior Jesus Christ brought me to a place of overcoming these pains of my past. It is to tell you how He helped me know He loves me. It is my prayer that it will also help you get to know yourself and God, and that He understands. You have a place in Him. Know that He is here for you and that He loves you. Stand still and let Him touch you. Let Him heal you. Take this journey with Him; you too will see that it is all in the journey with Jesus for you. In talking with other women, some of them my family members, others I had the pleasure of working in ministry with over the years, some I am still closely acquainted with. I have found that there are several distinct reactions to being abused.

As you read, try to identify which reaction you had or are still having; you may have over one reaction that you are dealing with so that you will better know how to deal with the issues that you are facing or have faced as you come to a complete understanding on how to overcome your hurt and pain to go to a place of peace with yourself and the people who have hurt you. Yes, you will come to a point where the person who has abused you is still alive or around you will have to learn to forgive and love them. Remember that forgiveness is something that we all need and what we must give to others. The Bible says in the familiar passage called the Lord's prayer that states, "And forgive our debts, as we forgive our debtors." Matthew 6:12 NKJV. We must forgive those who hurt us, those who abused us. We must forgive them so that we can be whole, so that we can be delivered and set free. One common reaction to childhood sexual abuse is to shut down completely. This results from so many traumas being suffered that the brain causes the individual to shut down emotionally totally and to forget the abuse for a time completely.

As a result, these people meander through life performing their daily tasks talking with others, and on the outside, seem to have it all together. Still, the truth is those people are so detached emotionally that they are almost always in and out of relationships. They don't trust *or* let *many* people be close to them; they have a defense mechanism. When someone has been severely hurt, it causes what I like to refer to as an open wound, and as with all scars, they can only get better when treated. The scars from abuse, incest, rape, and many other cases of abuse cause a blemish in our mind, a hole in our heart, and trauma that can live in the body for years just out of reach of our conscious mind we don't even know about.

As a result, those who have been abused can appear to have things all together when it is far from reality. They have perfected the art of looking happy and playing the well-rounded person role. They can often be overachievers in academics. They are usually extremely hard workers. They are very good at physical activities or the arts, and they more than likely spend a lot of time writing or reading. These allow the person to hide from the thoughts that run through their head daily, and it also keeps them from getting hurt again, or so they think. It is important to note and understand that a mind is a complex machine capable of holding large amounts of data and categorizing things so that each of us can adequately function in our daily lives. Just because someone looks like they have it all figured out doesn't mean that they do. This was me for many years. Always an overachiever striving to make sure that if and when I did something, I was the best at it or as close to the best as possible. Spending countless hours studying or reading, throwing myself into work. Taking on large amounts of responsibility that kept my mind occupied so that I would not think about my situation at home or the pain of my past.

In my opinion, more often than not, the person who seems like the one who has it all together can sometimes be more broken than the ones society deems as not having it together like drug addicts, prostitutes, thieves, and others that society deems undesirable. Do you want a dose of reality? The average drug addict, thief, fighter, or so-called unpleasant character is often more aware than those who look like they have it all together. They know they are broken. They know they are hiding from something in their life that they do not want to face. When I was doing drugs and drinking, I knew that. I was trying my hardest not to think about the abuse. I was self-medicating, trying with all that was in me to push out the pain, the hurt, the shame—trying to bury the feeling of hands touching me when I didn't want them—running from the memories that we constantly there. It became an art form to me, the ability to maneuver and manipulate my mind to a place that did not feel all the hurt and pain, or so I thought. I found later that I was only putting a bandage on a bleeding artery and if I wanted to be free from the pain; I was going to have to face it.

For me, the truth was the enemy had me so completely oppressed that I did not see what was going on until something that seemed minor or insignificant causes a catastrophic emotional breakdown. I started having nightmares, stopped sleeping, barely ate, and stopped doing any physical activity; in short, my life came to a complete standstill. Often people like me are plunged into depression and usually need some treatment to get them back on track. Yes, I said they need to get some help; if God did not want us to go to doctors, He would not have allowed men to become doctors. So, use some wisdom; if you need to get some help, then get some help. Let me establish this early in this book.

I am an Apostle, and I love God with all that I am and strive to represent him in all that I do. However, I am also a firm believer in the understanding that if you have a mental health issue; you need to seek mental health treatment. Everything is not demonic or the devil, or the enemy. Some things are just what they seem, an illness or sickness that requires medical intervention. So, if you are encouraged to go to the doctor for your physical issues, why are you afraid and often discouraged by the church to get your mental problems treated as well? If you need therapy, then please get it. If you want someone with a Christian background, then seek a Christian counselor; they are out there and understand that your faith is of the utmost importance to you and will help you deal with some things that you may face because of the trauma you experienced.

From my experiences, I have also found that another type of reaction is the person becomes withdrawn. If they are a child and still in school, their grades plummet, they get into fights, and there is a complete behavior change. They would stop if they were outgoing. If they were already quiet, they would become almost stoic. Often, they tend to wear clothes that are too big for them; they do whatever it takes to draw attention away from them. This was me as well. I told you it can show in combinations. They drink, smoke, and do drugs. Sometimes they act out, they mistreat others, and they can become bullies. If the child is young, the signs are that they wet the bed, withdraw from activities, and can mask the pain that they are experiencing by acting out physically and sexually at a very young age. I did all these things, anything I could do to stop the memories from flooding in. I started taking all kinds of pills and tried to commit suicide.

For some of these people, including myself, if they fail, they will usually try again. I tried again at least 4 times throughout my journey until I was completely healed. They will begin to self-harm with behaviors such as cutting themselves; they may develop an eating disorder. They will have frequent physical ailments, like headaches, stomachaches, and sore throats. There are physical manifestations of what they are trying to hide emotionally. The enemy also has this person believing that no one understands what they are going through. He wants them to think that they are alone. He is the only one there for them. Some individuals have no sexual preference. They become indiscriminate with whom they engage with. Unfortunately, some individuals can become abusers themselves, like my family. The adults in my life were abused and mistreated as children.

Because of what they experienced, they perpetuated the same cycle with their children and grandchildren; as a result, there are members of my family who themselves became abusers. I know because I too followed the same pattern.

I was highly abusive to my first husband. We would constantly get into physical altercations, and I genuinely feel the reason I could not fully be in my marriage fully is because of the hurt I experience in combination with the reason I married him. I did not marry this person for love. I married him so that I would not have to deal with the things that my mother was doing sexually to me. For peace of my mind and to keep from losing it all together, I hurt someone else. I vowed I would not be like my father and mother, yet I turned into an abusive person the first time I was married. Instead of ending the cycle, I continued it until I realized what was going on and understood that I could not continue to live my life the way those who abused me did.

My first marriage ended not because of him, but because I realized I would continue to perpetuate a cycle of hurt and abuse if I stayed married. My husband and I were young, and both came from abusive households, so I walked away not for his sake but for my own. I was not ready to be a wife, and I knew I was still broken mentally and emotionally, and I needed to be healed and whole to be the best partner to anyone else that came into my life. My motives for marrying him were all wrong and I couldn't do that to him. He deserved better than me, someone seeking to end their own hurt and pain by inflicting it on someone else.

And finally, there is the entirely hyperactively sexual personality. Me again, these people become highly promiscuous they engage in risky sexual behavior. It was almost as if sex was a game to me. Sexual preference was not an issue, and I have found from talking and ministering to so many like me, both male and female, that they can be heterosexual, bisexual, homosexual, pansexual and any other name you want to call it. They will have sex with anyone and anything. Sometimes, they have sex with multiple partners at the same time. They rarely use any protection, so they can sometimes have multiple kids, whether men or women. The goal of this person is not the sex itself it is to numb the hurt and pain, to seek affection physically hoping having another person in their life will fix the hurt they experienced psychologically. I have found some who have expressed that they cannot concentrate on anything for long periods. They tend to jump from job to job. Sometimes they can be very resistant to authority others are extremely sociable; they try to always please everyone they are around. Some of them become neat freaks. They clean their house almost religiously. They don't like anything out of place; they must always be in control. They must know the ends and outs of everything.

They do not if they have kids let them out of their sight for more than a few moments. This was me as well, extremely hypervigilant. They can be very harsh disciplinarians. When they feel threatened, they can overreact. They can have very addictive personalities. They can easily be hooked on drugs and alcohol as well. This is the type of personality that the enemy has influenced to do the most damage to themselves. Sex is often used as currency. They do not value themselves or their bodies because the abuse took that from them, so they do not care what they do, and the enemy sits back and enjoys toying with them.

Now I know that earlier I said that we often blame things on the enemy that should not be attributed to him alone, and that is true. However, understand this: the enemy can use the hurts and trauma that you carry to influence you to do things that you otherwise would not do because he can use the memories and feelings from those experiences to keep you bound to them.

So, while he may not have caused the hurt, he can manipulate it to suit his own need to keep you bound so that you have a stunted relationship or no relationship with God and others because of the scars that you carry from the trauma. Be aware that the devil is very real, and he will use whatever means he can to keep you from reaching the full potential and assignment that God placed you here to do. I do not attribute all things to him because some things are not attributed to him. Still, I know supremely that he is a master manipulator and the prince of the air, using everything he can to keep us away from God and His forgiving love and power.

Questions:

1. *Think about the person who abused you. Have you forgiven them? Do you think you will ever forgive them? Write your forgiveness statement*
2. *What reaction did you have to the abuse you suffered? Are you still having personality problems from the abuse?*

Pray and ask God to forgive you. Help you forgive those who have hurt you.

Turning Negative Effects Positive

Let's get to how this affects every aspect of your life. First, know that Jesus is the only solid foundation that you have. There is no man, no pill, no matter what you think: no doctor, no psychic, no shaman, no friend, no bottle of alcohol, no amount of cocaine, no meth, no crack, just Jesus Christ can get you through the entire healing process. I am not saying do not get help to deal with this. If I were, that would defeat the purpose of this writing this book, God allows people to become doctors so that people can be helped. What I am saying is that you must understand that if you don't learn to lean on God and rely on the Holy Spirit, then you have some dark days ahead. There are going to be some hard times ahead, but if you have Jesus Christ and the Holy Spirit, then they won't seem so difficult, for he will carry you when you can no longer walk, and he will protect you when the storm seems to be too much. By all means if you need medication, then take it. Some people need medication to deal with the things that has happened to them, and besides that, I, at some points in my life, had to take medication as well. God gives us enough sense to know that we may need some outside help.

What I am saying is that relying on medication alone will not make all the the difference, you will also need to talk to someone about the things that you have suffered as well. I went to therapy for years, but I was not ready to heal. I found that trust was so hard for me I was not receptive to opening up to someone. I spent years simply playing games with my therapist. I would say some of the most shocking things because I wanted to see their reaction. I wanted them to be shocked and appalled. I wanted them to ponder whether I was telling the truth. It was for years a battle of wills me saying I want to see how far I can push someone before they cracked and them struggling to break through the wall that I had up.

However, you learn God is the ultimate answer to all you go through. He is the one that will help you through all your difficulties. He is also the one who will help you through all that you must process. You may need help from outside sources, but you must get a firm foundation in faith and belief that God is real, that Jesus Christ died for your sins, that the Holy Spirit is your comforter and the reason for your being he is the difference-maker. Why would I seek help, then resist it? The answer is complex for me. I did not see life as others did.

Once the initial trauma happened, I viewed my world through traumatized lenses. Everything I did was through the scars of trauma. My view was blocked; I could not see myself or God in the proper context. I saw life with tainted eyes. Through the thoughts and ideas that I experienced from trauma; I ordered my surrounding. To me, everyone and everything was an enemy. I would ask myself how a therapist can help me when they aren't smart enough to realize that I am toying with them. That mentality was not just with counseling. It was also the same with God. I saw God as a big kid who sat on his throne and toyed with humans. The only redeeming value God had for me was that I knew him to be cruel, demanding, wanting me to serve Him freely, but never doing a thing to help me deal with the issues I had in my life. I blamed God for everything. He was my enemy at one point, and I wanted nothing to do with Him for any reason. So even though I knew I needed help, I still did not trust God, nor did I trust any human being to help me, either.

The key for me was first to acknowledge that I needed help, and then I had to be willing and receptive to that help to reach complete wholeness and healing from the abuse I endured all my life. Why me, GOD? That was the first question I had. Why did this have to happen to me? Why didn't you stop it? Why did you let them hurt me? Why weren't you there for me? What did I to deserve what they did to me? For a long time, I blamed God for what happened to me. I wanted nothing to do with God. I just wanted to drink, smoke, do drugs, have unprotected sex, and waste my life away. I have since found out that the things that happened in my life were not just to torture me or cause me pain for no reason, but the things that God helped me live through were not for me but for others who went through the same thing I went through. Some people are grossly affected mentally, to the point their cognitive function is vastly affected and has gone through less than I have. The level of trauma does not dictate whether you are psychologically stable or your cognitive functions are not adversely affected. It is how the mind can process and deal with the trauma. Some cannot connect with anyone or anything, emotionally or physically.

It took a long time for me to realize and see that God was there; it was God who kept me in my right mind. I could endure it because of God. The reason wasn't apparent to me for years, not until I had a relationship with God indeed. God knew I would not stay silent. He knew I would take all my experiences and tell others they would be ok. He knew I would go to war with the spirit of abuse and would let no one I encountered whom had been or was currently being abused must go it alone. He knew my assignment before the foundation of the world. He knew I would speak out against it and be a beacon in the emotional and physical storm that abuse victims experienced. God knew, I would lead them to Him. Not just superficially, but I would help anyone who asked for help to see Him and get to know Him, not just religiously, but relationally. That confidence He had in me was the catalyst of change in my life and the lives of others around me. He also knew that I would be stubborn, rebellious, curious, demanding, hungry for knowledge of Him.

He knew I was a fighter, and the experiences I faced, I would fight to come out for the better and not be bitter. I am not the only one. There are those of us who refuse to live as victims and refuse to let others live as victims. Instead, we will always help those who must deal with trauma from abuse. That realization for me was what changed things. I am a helper and a giver. I show the love of the Father to others or try to in all that I do. I want others to be whole, healthy, and free from the memories and scars of abuse and will fight for them sometimes harder than they fought for themselves.

First, I want you to understand that you want and need some answers about yourself if you are reading this. You want to know why you were abused? Why did GOD let this happen to you? To answer these questions is difficult, but I will try to encourage you as you go through your recovery. You are first an overcomer, not a victim. You have overcome what happened to you. If not, you would not be reading this. You already know that you can make it through anything since you made it through being abused. I have realized that if Jesus Christ did not love me, the Holy Spirit did not dwell in me and was not there for me to lean on, then I would never make it. The dreams, the flashbacks, the reliving, a life of torment can only be dealt with by trusting and leaning on GOD.

If you are reading this and feel as if GOD abandoned you, I am here to tell you He has always loved you and is still there waiting for you to let him in. I am here to encourage you by letting you know Jesus brought me through the abuse, the anger from the abuse, and the depression. Because He did it for me, I know He will do it for you as well. He will help you through the anger, depression, and feelings of doubt that often result from the abuse.

I cannot tell you how many times I asked God, why me? And each time, I felt as if God did not answer me This was frustrating for me because I wanted to know why there were people who went to church every Sunday and all during the week. They said that they loved God and were doing his will. I needed to know why God didn't stop them from hurting me. Why was I made to suffer? Then I saw why me over the years as I matured in God and as I walked in a prophetic anointing, there were people placed in my life that would ask me, have you ever been through something that was so hard that you feel lost and like you do not know if you will make it? In those moments of sharing some things that I have gone through, God answered me. He let me know I went through all that I went through to help someone else get to a place in their life where they can move past the pain and the hurt of their past. God said to me, "You are the vessel that I chose to expose the darkness and pain that so many women and children keep hidden."

I refer to women a lot because we are the ones who are often expected to get over what we went through. However, I know that there are men who have also suffered sexual abuse and physical at the hands of someone in their life. Therefore, I can understand both sides. Men feel ashamed and often feel like no one would understand what they went through. They lash out sometimes and cannot connect with others because they feel like what has happened to them is like a billboard that they carry around with them. It is also harder for men to realize that it is okay for them to feel the pain and mental anguish that comes from being abused, and they need to know that they can talk to someone as well. Please understand I am not an expert in these matters; I am simply a person who has the same type of story as many other people, both male and female, and I have had the profound pleasure of helping them reach their next level. However, I found that with the men that I have been able to speak with and support that they often felt excluded from the conversation of healing and restoration. Often for men, there is a built-in stigma associated with abuse.

A man is supposed to be strong mentally and physically. They are the leader in relationships and the leader in their home. They are expected to lead the household, set the discipline to be the provider. The Men that I have been blessed to speak with would often say to me it is hard to even open up about the abuse because of those types of stigmas; however, they needed and wanted to heal.

Anyone who has been abused and hurt needs someone to let them know they can talk about it and tell them they are not alone as well God has given me a unique perception in that I realize it is not a straightforward task to deal with the past. Still, if we do not, we cannot move to a place where the future that God wants us to have is attained.

So, in answer to the question, why me, God? I want you to know that everyone has free will, and some people choose to do the wrong things because they let the enemy guide them and not the Holy Spirit. I know it hurt to be abused and that you still carry the scars, but know this God saw you through all you went through. The first time I was told something to that effect, I said, why didn't he stop it instead of letting it happen? God gave me the strength to make it through all the things that I suffered for the first 13 years of my life. It has been God who helped me through 27 years of hurt and abuse from my mother and it has been God who has healed me from a lifetime of church hurt and abuse. He gave me the courage and the strength to keep seeking him, even through the abuse I suffered in my teen years through adulthood. Why? Will always be the question, but let me first help you understand why? The short answer is why doesn't matter. Apostle, what do you mean the why doesn't matter? The why does not matter because, at that point, the why becomes a roadblock to your healing and deliverance.

I spent years on the why with no better understanding of what I endured and understood because I was stuck at why. The definition of why is for what reason or purpose., expressing surprise or indignation, used to add emphasis to a response. And a basis or explanation.

Let's break it down when we ask why we ask what the reason was? We seek a rational explanation that we think will somehow help us understand the experience and the outcome. We are searching for cause and effect. What did we do to make this happen? What could we have done differently? If we did this, would the incident still occur? What are the variables? Was the outcome as expected? Seeking the why for me turned into a way to validate that the abuse was my fault. Something that I did caused my abusers to abuse me. You may have the same feelings and questions like you weren't good enough; maybe you could have been more loving, you could have been more obedient if the abuse happened in childhood the why causes you to blame the abuse on yourself as if there is something that you could have done differently that wouldn't have led to the abuse.

As a child, I would try to hide. I told other adults, ran away, and tried to commit suicide because of why. I ended up in a cycle that would last well into my adulthood. When I faced a situation like a flat tire on the side of the road, not enough money to pay my bills, or not being promoted on my job, I would analyze the why. Does this sound familiar? "If I didn't go down the road this way, my tire would not be flat?"

If I had taken that left instead of the right, I wouldn't have gotten into this accident, if I saved more money or didn't buy this or that I would have the money to pay my bills, If I worked harder and didn't take as much time from work or to complete the work duties assigned to me then I would have gotten the promotion. Of course, it does because we, as humans, always want to know that there is an explanation for what we experience.

Abuse causes a disconnect to our emotional and mental understanding. Remember, we are operating through trauma, so everything we see, or experience, is viewed through that lens., so asking why only leads to us continuing to abuse, torture, and torment ourselves. The abuser no longer has to you have become your abuser, seeking to blame yourself because of how you perceive yourself looking through the colored lens of abuse. I look back and know that God let me keep my mind. It was the love and protection of Jesus and the Holy Spirit that carried me. Once I came to this, understanding the why was no longer relevant. It took years for God to show me I could not move forward because I was too busy analyzing days long past for a reason and explanation to address the events of my life both spiritually and naturally. Seeking the why caused me to be stagnant and stuck. I could not move forward because I was too busy finding some reason for the abuse.

For years I went over and over in my mind the things that I could have done differently, going through every scenario wondering if a different choice would have garnered a different result. I became stuck on the why, and if I was stuck on the why, I could never move beyond the abuse. I learned the why wasn't necessary. It was just another way for me to stay in my torment long after my abusers had forgotten about the things they did. They slept at night while I lay awake, questioning why. Once God showed me, I was getting stuck at why I could see the pattern of behavior that led to my destructive and self-derogating way of thinking. Once the why was moved out of the equation, understanding healing and forgiveness of myself and those who harmed me was easier to attain.

I know that is not the answer you wanted, but that is the only answer I can give you. I know Jesus loves me and that He helped me to get beyond it. GOD wants us to know that he is the ultimate healer and our salvation strength leader and guide.

The BIBLE says in Romans the eighth chapter that we are more than conquers and that we cannot let anything separate us from the love of GOD. Wanting to know why was separating me from the love of God, I was so busy looking for the cause that I could not see the solution. I was so caught in my mind in the darkness of the thoughts and self-loathing that I could not truly see my savior and redeemer. Even though I knew of him, I did not honestly know him because I never let him in. The why kept him out. That constant question kept me from seeing His love for me. It kept me from healing. I stood in my way as much as I wanted to blame the devil, demons, the enemy. It was not him that stood in the way of my healing; I stood in my way. I put up roadblocks; I sabotaged my deliverance because I saw myself through trauma-filled eyes. Ultimately, I sacrificed my redemption and happiness because I could not let go of the why. So, I found I needed and wanted to heal, and for that, I needed to trust God. I had to know what that meant.

That means there is nothing too hard for our God to solve, and there is no situation that he cannot provide relief and shelter through. Jesus knows who we are, what we suffered, and what we must go through. Jesus was there when you were being hurt. He was there when you were alone and crying. When you were angry, he was there when you went through all you had to go through. God knew who you were from the foundation of the world. He knew what you would go through and what you would suffer and what you would accomplish. Remember, man has free will, and man will do what he wants to do when I say man, I mean women as well because contrary to popular opinion, women can be abusers as well.

What God does is equip us to go through what we must help others to go through what they have to, in order to help others, make it. For example, a young man who lived in a beautiful family had all the finer things in life, could go to the finest schools, and had all that he needed. Then he has a tragedy in his family his mother becomes ill. she suffers tremendously; she is in constant pain; she becomes withdrawn, sad; she is on countless medications to stay alive. Often, she cries, and even sometimes he hears her wish for death. This impacts him so much so that he wishes there is something he can do to make her better.

He says that if he could, he would help her. Eventually, after years of suffering, his mother dies, and he feels powerless. This young man grows up missing his mother. Everything that he does in his life, from her death, leads to a greater purpose in his life. In school, he studies harder. he reads every material he can get in the medical profession. He soon becomes a doctor specializing in treating patients with cancer, then he helps other people who have the same illness as his mother had. His patients have a compassionate doctor who can help them. I say that the young man in the example had a tragedy in his life. He used the pain of that experience to let it motivate him to go to school, go through all that he needed to become a doctor to grow up and help other people whom God ordained for him to help.

Now let us look at another example: there is a little girl who loves her mother very much. She goes everywhere mommy goes; she wants to be just like her when she grows up. Her mother is giving her all to her job. She watches her mother have compassion for everyone and knows that her mother will always be there to protect her, no matter what she faces. Then the unthinkable her mother's boyfriend does something so horrifying that the little girl is shattered because of it. He touches her inappropriately, molests her, and threatens that if she tells, he will kill her mother, whom she loves with all her heart. The little girl becomes withdrawn, and as time passes, she stops doing the things she used to.

She wets the bed. She acts out in school. Finally, her mother asks her what is wrong. She gets the courage to tell what he is doing to her, but her mother blames her to the child's dismay. She tells the little girl if you didn't flirt with him and didn't always want to be around him. If you weren't always sitting on his lap or wanting to be left at home alone with him, then this wouldn't have happened.

At that moment, the little girl's world has shattered the mother that is supposed to love and protect the one she was protecting by not telling because she didn't want the man to harm her has just blamed her for the abuse and said to her it was her fault. As the little girl grows up, she skips school. She gets in fights. She is angry all the time. Her mother marries the man that is abusing her. The young girl realizes that her mother doesn't care about her and does not protect her. The child grows into a teen and is promiscuous. She drinks, does drugs, seeks love and validation from other sources, but nothing fills the void. The girl becomes a woman. All her hopes and dreams are gone. She constantly fights with her mother, who says that she doesn't understand why she acts the way she does. The young woman leaves home, runs away frequently, becomes involved with an unsavory crowd. She is raped and beaten by her boyfriend, and she accepts it because she remembers her mothers' words. She must have deserved the abuse she suffers in silence. One day, her mother becomes sick and reaches out to her, asking her to help her. The now bruised and battered young woman says no. She stays away, battling in her mind with the memories that she carries like a weight around her neck.

The mother dies, and the woman doesn't even seem to care. She is lost and in despair, and eventually, she gives in and allows herself to fall into despair. She has no will or wants to live, and ultimately, she succumbs to death from drugs.

In comparison, the young woman affected by trauma and abuse spends her life trying to bury the hurt and mask the pain of the abuse and her mother's betrayal and denial. She never reaches the purpose and potential that God desired and designed her for. She never gets over the hurt. She spends her life masking the pain. Even though she is desperate for relief, the trauma and betrayal cause her to think that no one cares; therefore, she never reaches out for help, and she does not accomplish the assignment that she was initially created to do.

What is the difference between the two? The young man is nurtured and protected and shown love and affection. The pain of losing his mother pushes and motivates him to be a great success. because of the values his mother instilled in him, he sees the world through unclouded eyes and sees opportunities at every turn to better himself and those around him. The young woman saw life; differently, she saw the world through the trauma she experienced. She does not trust anyone because the person who was supposed to protect her didn't and that abandonment, hurt, and trauma is instilled in her. The phrases it was your fault that she was to blame, in conjunction with marrying the perpetrator and continually exposing the young child, have lasting effects. She hears and sees life through that hurt and trauma. She can never get beyond thinking that she deserved the abuse because she was told. These two examples show the difference in seeing life through love and trauma and how each can affect an individual.

This is what I mean when I say that God has permitted us to go through certain things to use what we have gone through to help others go through what they need to. Now, did God allow the young woman to suffer? The answer is No. God does not sit and intentionally let someone suffer. It is not God sitting picking you out saying I want this one to suffer, so I will ignore her cries for help and not help her through this.

Man has free will, and some people choose to use that free will for selfish, destructive, and massively misguided reasons, inflicting pain on others. The young woman was wounded, but God always has a means of release and escape. The issue was not that God wasn't there, it was that because of the hurt and abuse, the young woman could not see Him reaching for her, wanting her to know He loved her and that He was there to comfort her.

The issue wasn't and isn't that God does not care when we are hurt, but rather, we can't see Him or reach Him genuinely when we are looking through clouded lenses of trauma and hurt. He is there. We just need someone to show us how to accept Him and trust Him to heal us. Let's look at me. For example, I was abused most of my childhood and part of my adult life sexually, physically, emotionally, and verbally. As a result of that abuse, I wanted to shut down. Instead, I grow more assertive every day because I know that Jesus Christ lives in me through the Holy Spirit. I spend most of my days talking with other women who have been abused.

I spent the last several years writing this book to help others. Did I always feel that way? No, I went through a period where I wanted nothing to do with God. Why would I want to serve a God who let the abusers in my life hurt me? Why would I lean on a God who would not reach down and instantly wipe all of them off the face of the earth? I went to church every day sometimes during my childhood, and not once did this God help me, or so I thought. He didn't stop the beatings, rape, molestation, emotional and verbal abuse. They were able to use me and hurt me. He let every man who touched me from a baby live. He let them do the things they did to me. What would I ever want or need from a God who did not even care? If he cared, he would have saved me.

For a long time, God was the enemy to me; therefore, I could not receive His love or healing. I didn't see Him as my help and strength; I didn't see him as my comforter or my redeemer. I saw Him as a deity who toyed with human beings and didn't care how much we suffered. I now understand that my view of God was tainted by the people who hurt me. My parents were both ministers, my uncles, aunts, grandparents, cousins, and everyone in authority over me was in some ministry capacity. I started in ministry early singing, then teaching Sunday school and the choir, and traveled to minister all before the age of 12, but I did not trust the God I sang and ministered about. How is that possible? I saw God through a tainted lens; I saw God through the trauma inflicted on me, not for who He really is. Slowly, the God I sang and ministered about became tangible to me. I sought Him because I wanted to understand why He didn't help me. The more I studied and the more I prayed, begging God to help me.

At first, it was small. I took tentative steps towards the God I feared and disliked because he didn't fix it. He didn't stop the abuse, the rapes, the trauma, the pain, and the memories, so going to Him in sincerity was brutal because I had no reason to trust Him. He, as far as I was concerned, betrayed me, too. But God is patient, and God is loving, and even in my questioning, He kept His hands on me. I soon started praying out of anger and desperation and wanted God to explain himself and answer the charges I levied against Him. God was guilty in my eyes, guilty of betrayal, malice, cruelty, and destruction, so I approached Him at first in anger, demanding that he answer the charges.

Then one day, I cried; it was a cry deep in my bones. Everything in me cried out. I wailed and screamed. I broke mentally. In that moment, I cried, Jesus, help me! It was a deep, sincere cry. I needed relief from all the pain I carried. At that moment, lying on the floor of my bedroom, I felt a presence and peace. The God I levied charges against chose that moment when I was ready to give up on myself and life showed up. It was a still quiet voice, one phrase that changed my life from that moment "I am here." My soul wept, and again I heard, "I am here" I remembered that voice; it was the same voice I attended as an 11-year-old child. God chose that moment to show up, and my life has never been the same.

I started a support group in my local church so that other women and men who have been through this will have somewhere to go to talk about what they have been through and what effects it has had and is still having on their lives. So even though what happened to me was painful, I truly believe that Jesus is here for me and that he has given me the strength to tell my story as many times as I have to. So that others will not suffer in silence. That is what I mean by turning the negative that you have sustained into positive. Use it as a motivation to do great things for others and yourself.

Move beyond the pain into peace; let the Holy Spirit Comfort you through this so that you can lead someone else to Christ so that they too can be fully healed and restored and move on with their life and help someone else to get through their pain.

Questions:

1. *Have you asked God why you? Did you get an answer?*
2. *How can you help someone who has been through the same things you have?*

3. *Do you still have issues trusting God and if so, why or why not?*
4. *Do you see God as your enemy or your help and do you think that your view of Him will ever change?*

God's Love is enough

Let us inspect why love is so essential. Beloved, let us love one Another love is of God, and everyone who loves is born of God and knows God. He who does not love does not know God, for God is love. In this, the love of God was manifested towards us, that God has sent his only begotten son into the world, that we might live through him. In this is love, not that we loved God, but that he loved us and sent his son to be the propitiation for our sins. I John 4:7-10. What do these scriptures mean basically, God is love now that is deep the everlasting, omnipotent, omnipresent, infinite God is love that means that love is ceaseless. It is limitless. There is always something there. It will never change. Love is without fault. You will see that no matter what you have gone through in this life, Jesus will always protect and love you. The Father is love, so to be His is to be loved by Him. He created you out of love and only desired to give you the love He has for not just you for all. Think about it, God, who can end the world In the blink of an eye, a being can open the earth and instantly swallow thousands. A fierce, powerful, fantastic force that created all that you see and know, The God who formed, the world desires one thing, and that is to love us and desires nothing but for us to show that love to the world so that those who may not know Him will want to know Him based on the love that you show them because that is how they know and understand who He is. Think about it. Let it sink in there is someone out there that loves you for you, not the mask that you put on or the walls that you put up, but because he created you, he loves you. He died for you. He left the comforter to be there for you; with his help you will succeed. It is what he desires for all his children, knowing this can be very difficult for the abused person to grasp, however, with prayer and with the help of an excellent support system. I know you will fully know and understand that God loves you. When someone is abused, particularly at a young age, the issue of trust becomes a big factor. Because of mistrust is hard for an abused person to understand the concept of unconditional love, especially the type of love that God shows us. When you feel unworthy, or you feel as though you are unlovable, which usually occurs when you have suffered any abuse, some tend to feel that they are unlovable, so the concept of God loving us is hard to comprehend. It is my prayer that as you read this book, if nothing else you learn God is love, and it is His love that makes the most significant impact on your life and how you view Him and others around you.

Food for thought if the abuse happened when you were a child, particularly if the abuse was repeated by a close family member or family friend that the child trusts. That child could develop and typically deals with issues of trust because of that trauma. And any form of abuse is shocking and so traumatizing that the child suffered inner shame and extreme humiliation and guilt and pain and depression. They may at first have a difficult time believing that God loves them.

Not that there is something wrong with that person. It is just that they have been hurt and violated by someone who told them they love them, so they cannot at first fully accept the notion that someone anyone can love them. Because you have been so badly injured by the person you loved and trusted, we could not trust that Jesus loves us, so, therefore, we tend to think that we cannot be loved or give love completely.

The thing that I find I went through was that because I was hurt and abused at such a young age and it happened for so long, and it was done by people who said that they loved me, that they were only doing what was right by me, my concept of love became misguided. I looked at love instead of it being something that I wanted in my life; it became something that I was too afraid to acknowledge and something that I did not want. The result was that because I felt unloved by my family and others, I could not get it through my head that God loved me. I always thought that I deserved what I got from those around me. I was constantly being told that no one loved me, and no one wanted me, not even my mother, and for me, I felt that since my mother didn't love me enough to keep me, how could God love me? There was also the fact that God did not stop the abuse that made me feel like he didn't love me or want me.

I didn't understand why he didn't help me, why he didn't make them stop. I would say if you are God, why are they still hurting me, and why won't you make them go away? The anger I felt only made my need to understand love more natural. I was desperate for an explanation, but I could not find one, so for a while, I decided I didn't need love.

The way I felt about love was soon changed when I was 30 years old. The baby I just gave birth to was my second child. When they left me alone with him for the first time, I looked at him. I held him close. I closed my eyes as tears fell. Never had I felt such raw emotion, such fear and wonder. All at the same time, I wanted to hold him forever, shelter him, keep him safe. I prayed that no harm ever come to him. I tried to protect him from the world. That is when I realized how much God loved me, that love was possible, and that love was not fake. It is real, and it is achievable.

You may wonder why it took so long for me to grasp the concept of unconditional love; the answer is that until the moment I held my baby in my arms, I could not fully understand the dept of love and how it manifests in people's lives. All I wanted at that moment was to protect, nurture, and shield him from everything that I had experienced as a child and even into my adult life. I did not want him to face the same obstacles that I did; I wanted a better life for him, emotionally and physically. I didn't have a lot of money and didn't have a big bank account or a home to call my own, but what I had and still carry was a desire to make his life peaceful and full of hope: joy and wonder as I could.

When his brother was born 15 months later, I found my heart stretched larger and wider for him as well. Love seemed to grow within me as my children grew. I have vowed to be the best mother and teacher that I can be. I reinforced the values that I have learned over the years into them. I constantly told them I loved them and adopted the concept of allowing my children to have an open dialog with me so that they were supported in every decision they made and still do to this day. In doing so,

I have shown my children the very essence of the Love of God through the love and appreciation that I show them daily.

Isaiah 54:10 talks to each of us on this wise Jesus is saying as large as mountains are they may fall, and all of the hills that are around may crumble his love for us is unfailing and unconditional Jesus will no matter what always be there and always love us. With prayer and faith and some excellent support, all people who have been abused or abused in the past can overcome all obstacles. Another point to consider is that people in your life may need to be removed. During this process, you need to be in the presence of those people who will constantly remind you that Jesus loves you and that they love you, too.

During this walk, there are people you may need to distance yourself from, not because you dislike or hate them. But because you need to have supportive people around you who will be there for you when times get difficult for you emotionally. Having a person who has a negative attitude who is constantly telling you they don't see how you made it through all that you did it gets into your mind that maybe you can't make it. When the seed of negativity is planted, it is harder for you to see God's love clearly, so for that reason, step away from those people. One of the easiest ways to stay stuck in the mode of feeling as though you are a victim and not worthy of being loved is staying around people who constantly remind you of the hurt and trauma you suffered. For instance, I lived with my mother for a few reasons one my health, and because I knew that she too had been abused, so I stayed to show her love and hoped that she could see the love of God through me.

That decision caused me years of oppression; why do I say that? The answer is simple: I needed and wanted something from my mother that she could not give, and that was love and support. Even though I supported her, she could not reciprocate that love for me. She spent days reminding me of the past and the abuse, telling me things like I must have liked it, or I would not have stayed. I must have looked forward to being raped or molested because I would have told more people if I didn't. For years, my mother convinced me or tried to convince me that the abuse was something I invited and wanted.

The hurt that this caused me was devastating, and for years I believed her; otherwise, I would have had to face the reality that she abused me. I took it as she was trying to help me at first, until my concept of unconditional love changed, and I saw God differently. After that, I saw that, in fact, it was my mother who did not understand love and that she was comfortable hurting others around her because she was hurt. The abuse my mother suffered caused her to be narcissistic and a bully. She found ways to tear down any sincere relationship I had with God. It was hard because my mother insisted on dragging me to church every Sunday and forced a relationship with God from when I was sixteen.

I was not happy with God, so being forced to go to church only made me resent church and religion. However, I must thank her for that because she constantly took me to church and continuously quoted the bible to me. I started seeking God for myself. At first, it was to understand what I faced as a child, and later it turned to how she made me feel. Crying out to God in my desperation because of her emotional and physical abuse and other abuse forms caused the opposite. Instead of hating God, I developed a relationship with Him. I saw God for myself and understand how the experiences in my life could help others. Showing them that God is love because I can tell my story and reach those that people in the church may not reach. After all, they do not have a personal understanding of what abuse does to an individual and how much help they need. I learned through this journey that some will need to hear others' stories about how they overcame so that they would know they can overcome. The bible says we overcome by the blood of the lamb and by the word of our testimony-Revelations 12:11 (a) what does this mean? Simply this: some cannot overcome what they have experienced unless some will tell their struggles, triumphs, and failures during their journey. Seeing someone else who has experienced the same traumas or abuse that you went through and watching them come out of it success-fully gives them the motivation needed to know that they can and will overcome it.

For me, that is the goal not only to share my story but to shed a little light at the end of a dark corridor, letting you know it will not always be dark. You will not always live with the emotional pain and hurt from the trauma, but that one day, you too will overcome, and you can then help someone else to overcome.

Questions:

1. *Do you really know that Jesus loves you?*
2. *Are there some people that you need to remove from your life? If so, who are they?*
3. *What type of abuse did you suffer? Are you ready to deal with it?*
4. *Pray to ask the Lord to help you understand his love for you. Ask him if there are people you need to remove from your life. Ask him to help you deal with the abuse you suffered.*

Do I really trust Him?

Let's go back to how you feel about trust. Most people who have been abused, have an unfortunate sense of distrust. Often, we have built a wall around ourselves. We thing that the wall that we have built is impervious to other people. We make sure that we keep people at arm's length and make sure that they do not get too close. This is a defense mechanism often employed by people who have been abused. The concept or thinking behind it for me was if you cannot get to me the authentic me, then you will not be able to hurt me to other people. This wall is impenetrable, or so we think. We try to keep all our feelings, whether good or bad, bottled up inside. You usually don't associate yourself with other people; however, you could also be on the opposite end of the scale, where you are always laughing and smiling whenever someone sees you, yet deep inside you feel as if you could just die. What is your authentic self? To answer that, we must start with the word authentic. Authentic is defined real or genuine, not copied, or false. True and accurate. So, your authentic self is the real and genuine you. It is you that is how you see yourself and how you feel it is the personification of you, the person in all your glory, good or bad.

It is the part of yourself that you do not let others see for any reason because that is all that you feel that you have left after trauma. Can your concept of self be flawed? Unfortunately, yes when trauma is introduced, especially at an early age when your idea of self is formed. The concept of self is how a person thinks, gauges, evaluates and even becomes cognizant of themselves, (Baumeister (1999). The concept of self is believed to be formed during early childhood, comprising two components the existential self, which is the understanding that a person is separate and distinct from others or their surroundings (Bea, 1999) and the categorical self, which is the understanding that we are a part of this world and begin to classify or designate ourselves into groups in relation to gender, age, ethnicity, etc. (Angela Oswalt, MSW, Gulf Bend Center, 2020). Since the concept of self forms during early childhood, usually between the ages of 2 to 7 years of age, trauma during that age has a significant impact on the person's concept of self and how they see themselves authentically. This is because when that type of trauma is introduced at an early age, the child then forms their sense of self through that trauma. It can take years to help that person separate their concept of self from the experience of trauma. To them, they are the same. The trauma becomes their self-concept or the way they perceive themselves to be.

So how do we that have been traumatized see our authentic self? We often see our authentic self as broken, worthless, bad, damaged, or less than. We decide that because we were abused or broken, that other see us as broken, so we hide that part of us away from everyone. We view the world as an enemy only there to hurt and harm, therefore, we throw up a wall to protect what we see as our authentic self. The concept of authentic self is then scarred by our experience. So how do we correct that and how do we view ourselves as complete and whole? First, we must understand, as I stated in this book earlier, that we need to explore all avenues for help so that we can become complete and whole. That is why I take issue with the church's narrative that all you must do is pray and God will make all things go away, the sad reality is that it's not that simple. There are some exceptions. Everything is not a demon or the enemy, some things must be treated and dealt with to be corrected abuse is one of them in particular sexual abuse that happens in early childhood. According to the Journal of Psychology 20-40% of those who have experienced childhood sexual trauma develops significant psychological issues (Journal of Psychology, 2019). These issues can be severe major depression, anxiety, depression, eating disorders, Post Traumatic Stress disorder etc, in order to help with these, you may need some sort of cognitive therapy to help you deal with those issues and combat some of the effects that they have on your everyday life. Yes, God was an essential part of my healing and recovery, but I too had to lean on other sources for help with dealing with the ramifications of being abused. I implore you to search yourself to determine if you feel that you need outside resources to help you. For each person, the journey is as different and varied as the individuals themselves, some need therapy, others rely totally on God and God alone to get through it. I am not saying that you must go to therapy. I am saying that for me I needed that component in conjunction with my Faith to retrain my thoughts and behaviors so that I could be a complete person and overcome the abuse since mine was very extensive and lasted for several years in early childhood.

Exactly what is trust? According to the Merriam-webster dictionary, trust means: Assured reliance on the character, ability, strength of someone or something. One in which confidence is placed. Now that says a lot once you have been molested or abused or raped, the first thing you lose is trust. Trust in human beings as a whole or in family members if that is who abused you. So, if you cannot rely on the character, ability, or strength, of people who you see every day. How can you be expected to fully trust God? I will tell you how to first look at what Jesus did for you before you even knew you were you. He gave his life for you. Look at all that he has done for you so far. You are alive, you wake up every morning; you have a job, or you have someone who is financially responsible for you, you eat every day. These are all things that Jesus provides and know that he is still there with his arms wide open to you. It may take some time but you must learn to trust Jesus with all your heart, start small talk to him every day like you would talk to a friend, read and studying his word, tell him you do not know how to trust him, tell him your doubts and fears, tell him how much you hurt. For me, I remember my first tentative steps toward trusting Jesus came from me speaking openly and frankly in prayer. Sometimes I would just say, ok God, I am having a hard time with this or when is this nightmare going to be over? Even questioning if He even cared that I was hurting or suffering. There were even those times when I approached Him in anger, saying if you cared and was there, this would not have happened. I worked through every emotion in prayer at first weekly and as my relationship with God deepened, and I understood Him more. I went to him in prayer more frequently until I talked with God daily, sometimes hourly when things got difficult. Approaching God in this way allowed for a solid relationship to form within me. I trusted that God was there and that He was directing my path. As I worked through counseling and different cognitive therapies, I also took those issues to God in prayer often to see if I was making the right decision. In ministry, I was being told that God can and will fix everything, but I was not led to believe that I could safely go to any sort of counselor or doctor, I was told that God will work it out if you have enough faith. This denoted that the reason that I had such difficulty coming to grips with the pain of my past was because my faith was not strong enough, so I believed I Needed stronger faith.

It has taken years for me to understand that God does not put those types of restrictions on it, man does. If you need a doctor, then go to a doctor to get intervention for your condition it is the same psychologically. If you need therapy, then do not be afraid to go to therapy just because it may be frowned upon in your local assembly. I am in no way saying that you must go the route I did. I am simply sharing with you my experiences and what helped me to overcome the abuse I suffered. For me, it was just that simple at first; I remember saying to God I am angry with you look what you let happen to me. How can you say you love me and all of this happened. I am scared that I will never be loved; I don't enjoy being around people, I just want to be left alone. I am angry because of what happened to me. But know this through it all. Jesus was still there for me. He still held out his hand to me, even when I felt empty on the inside. He held me when I wanted to take my own life; he held onto me and did not let me go. I learned to trust him slowly at first, but then as I got stronger in him, I learned. To trust him more. Even now I am still growing to trust him more and more each new thing I face helps me to trust him more. I know from the things I have read in the Bible that he did, the people he saved, the healings and miracles. I know I can rely on his character, ability, and strength. That is how I learned to trust him, and that is how you will learn to trust him too. Now not only do I trust Jesus, but I have also learned how to trust people again, I have learned to assess a person's character, ability, and strength. This allows me to consult God and trust that he will show me who I can trust.

One thing that most survivors have in common before they become overcomers is they have trouble in the area of trust. Think about it. Some of us sit in church all our lives and see others being helped delivered and set free. We hear the preacher teach about how much Jesus loves us and how much he is there for us; we want to believe, but because of the hurt that we have suffered, it is hard to make that first step to trust God.

An overcomer transcends or moves beyond distrust to trust to rely on God to understand that He is there for them to a new sense and awaking of themselves. Remember, this cannot be done alone. When you are a survivor as long as I was, I know you can stay in a survival mode for years; you wonder if you can go on each day. You get so used to living shells of existence; we get so used to having the walls up to not letting anybody in to holding on just by a strand, until one day you hit the wall and you feel defeated you feel lost and alone and afraid all over again this is when I realized that there had to be more, after years of sitting in church and not feeling anything, not sure of myself, not confident in my abilities, watching other people getting a breakthrough it came to me one Sunday while in church that I wasn't sure I really trusted God. When I searched myself and prayed for understanding, I went from being a survivor to an overcomer. It all began when I started trusting God. I said all of that to say this; you must learn to trust God. You may ask, how do I trust God and others, even myself? Yes, I said you must learn how to trust. Why is that? It is simple, really. Consider this from my personal experience while going through the sexual abuse I suffered. I analyzed why I felt I looked forward to it. My body responded to the abuse, even when I really didn't want it to. My body betrayed me. I thought, how can you be responding to this, so I lost trust in myself? I felt I couldn't trust my responses to anything. I stopped trusting in my instincts, my emotions, my feelings. I wondered if everyone who was sexually molested felt this way, and I felt stupid for even responding to the acts of sexual misconduct that I was enduring. It was during therapy that I learned that the body responds differently for everyone. however, there are some that the body responds to what is happening physiologically, meaning that the flesh responds to sexual assault and misconduct even when the mind hates and detests what is happening. This in no way means that you invited, wanted, or enjoyed the act itself. It means that physically the body responds the way it always responds to being touched in a sexual way.

This was a big revelation for me because I thought that because my body responded, then I must have liked or wanted what was happening to me. Physically, the body has an involuntary response to sexual contact. There are certain ways that we physically respond, and those responses are not differentiated from it being a sexual assault or pleasure. The body response even when the brain knows that what is happening is unwanted or asked for. So, for me, I needed to understand that what was physically happening was not related to giving consent for the abuse. They are totally separate. I understood through therapy that psychologically I was damaged and physically my body responded this did not mean that I could not trust my body, emotions, feelings, abilities, or cognitive function this meant that physically the body responds automatically to certain stimuli this was not consent and it was not my body betraying me. Once I learned this, I learned I could trust my feelings, abilities, emotions, and thoughts. I finally understood that what I grew up understanding about my spirituality and myself was flawed not because I was flawed but because the ones who taught me who God is were flawed in their teaching and understanding. The church has often brushed these types of issues under the rug. This is not because they want to it is because the church for years was not equipped to deal with these types of issues. It was out of sight, out of mind.

I have learned to incorporate this type of teaching into the ministries I deal with and oversee because the need for understanding of these issues is essential to the over-all spiritual growth and development of each member. We must learn as ministries to adapt to the changes and issues as they surface. This means that we need to understand each member and the issues that they have or are currently facing to help them as a whole mind, body, and spirit.

How do you learn to trust if you have never been taught that there may have been circumstances that caused you to not trust in the first place? Once that issue is address or brought to light then the person is better able to understand what is happening to them and why they have issues with trust in correcting the thinking about trust you open the door for the person to take the first tentative steps to trust God.

That is the first step you must believe that you can see Jesus, you can see him in nature, people, the miracle of birth, waking you up in the morning, the colors of a rainbow and the cool breeze that always seems to blow when you are hot and sticky. Trusting is a process of letting go; it is a sense, an act of faith. You need not pray for more faith, rather a strengthening of the faith that you already possess once this is established, then you can begin the process of trust. God wants you to trust him just like you assume that when you sit in a chair, it will hold you, and just as you think, the car will start whenever you crank it.

Jesus wants you to know that you can always lean on him. He wants you to tell him all your problems, and he wants you to know that coming to him will not get you punished, but rather will make you closer to him. Jesus wants you to let go of your anger, hurt, bitterness, and contempt for others, and step out from behind the wall that you have built for defense and protection. Let go of all memories and bad thoughts. Simply trust him, don't take the pain of abuse give it to Jesus.

One of things that we as a people do and it is in my opinion one of the biggest things that hinder our trust and faith in God, what we will do is pray and ask him to take away our pain or bless us financially or bless us with a husband or a wife, then if he does not do what you want him to do within a matter of days, then you take it back, trying to fix it yourself. Know this: if you could fix yourself, then tell me why Jesus would even die for our sins, or why would he give us the Holy Spirit to comfort us realistically if we could handle things yourself, we would have already.

Why have you been carrying around all that pain and guilt for so many years? God says that he will always be there and that he will never leave you nor forsake you; he tells you he is protecting you with his rod and his staff, comforting you. God is not a man who could or would lie. He can be believed and must be believed in, so that you can trust him and turn all your problems over to him to work out. Trust Jesus with all your heart and lean not unto your own understanding. Trust in the Lord for all things that this life may throw at you. Without belief, you cannot trust. Without faith, you cannot trust, and you can't move on if you don't learn to trust and lean on Jesus. I realized I had to trust someone in order to get help and since I had no faith or belief that any human being could help me; I was left to trust Jesus, and I tried to trust him, but I lived in my past, which dictated my present and therefore hindered my future.

Because I was stuck in the pain of the trauma I endured, I could not see and fully understand the God I said I served. I looked at God through the eyes of someone dealing with trauma, therefore every interaction I had with anyone, and even God, was clouded by that trauma. I approached God like He wasn't going to fix it because the ones who caused it couldn't fix it. No amount of I am sorry would have made it better. I needed to not see life through a broken lens. I needed to see clearly through the eyes of someone who was healed and whole, so how could I get there if I only saw God through the trauma I suffered? The only way was for me to understand what I was actually dealing with and how did the abuse manifest itself in my daily life and in my spiritual walk with God. Someone who I associated with in church told me God placed them in my life. They said that God told them I needed to talk to someone I trusted to get the feelings I had bottled up inside out. But for me, that was hard, for I trusted no one, not one person in this world. After being plagued for so many years by pain, depression, doubt, unworthiness, regret. I needed to empty some luggage; I needed to cut off some weights whether that meant people or memories.

The first person I attempted to speak with about this went and told everything that I spoke with them about to leaders in my church. This was a blow to me psychologically. I refused for years to try again. The hurt was too great from the hurt this person inflicted. When I first spoke to this person about some memories, a sense of relief came over me. It was as though a new me emerged. This process did not happen overnight. It took countless sessions with this person who was trained as a counselor to get me to where I could even trust them enough to release what I was holding. At first the sessions were superficial I would talk about the weather or current events and maybe at the end of the session I would say one thing that had to do with what I went through nothing serious it started with the statement "I was abused as a child". Why did I start there? At first, it was a way for me to test the person and gauge whether I could fully release to them. I watched their reaction to that revelation to see how they were going to handle what was said. The outcome would determine if I could really trust this person and if I could open up to them. Their response was at first shocking. They answered simply, "ok now that you have said that before we do anything else, I would like to pray with you". They did not ask any probing questions, did not look shocked or appalled, did not recoil from me instead they said let me pray with you.

The prayer was simple Father now that this your child has opened up about some of the deep issues in her heart give me the ability to listen and understand her position so that I will be able to help her deal with some feelings that she has about her past. And Father, if I am not worthy or am not the one who can help her, please show me, and direct me to a source that can and will help her. I am not saying that you need a Christian counselor. I'm saying you need someone whom you can talk to openly and freely without judgement and hinderance. For me, it was essential that the person who I spoke to understood that my spiritual walk was the only thing that kept me around for as long as it did. You make the choice if you need help or counseling of what is the best fit for you. It may take more than just reading this book.

This is not meant to take the place of any type of mental health counseling you may need. It shows you the journey that I took to get to where I am today. I needed both my Faith and belief in God and counseling to overcome the issues I faced from the abuse that I endured. That was all it took I understood at that moment even though this person may or may not have had the skills to help me they understood that my faith and belief in God was the center of my existence, it was the one constant that I could hold on to. My spiritual understanding of God and opening up to him was more relevant to my healing at that moment than the person's need or desire to help me.

They understood that in order to help me see things more clearly; I needed them to understand my belief and trust in God himself. The very act of that one prayer caused me to see them differently the fact that they did not immediately declare that they were going to be the one to fix me but that they too consulted God for direction on how to help me gave me the assurance that I could talk to them about my issues because I knew they were not going to just spout a bunch of psychobabble at me they understood that to heal my mind they would have to first help me to spiritually see and understand how all of it would work together for my greater good.

I believe that for me that was the only way I was going to cope with understand and overcome the pain of the traumas I faced as a child and even into my adult life. You chose your path and what works for you just know that in choosing to want to be healed and whole there is not a cookie cutter blanket way to go about healing it is as varied as the individuals themselves everyone does not heal the same or at the same rate and it doesn't mean that your faith is not strong enough nor does it mean that you do not believe that God can and will heal you it means that you may need other modalities to help you achieve that goal.

I asked God to purge me it was then that I realized I trusted him as well as myself because I knew God would only lead me in the right direction to the right people as I also read and meditate on scriptures that help me trust Jesus more, my faith grows stronger, my past stays in the past, my presence is brighter, and I now not only know, but feel that God holds my future.

Questions:

1. Do you understand what trust is?,
2. Do you trust Jesus?
3. Are you a survivor or an overcomer?
4. If you do not trust Jesus what would it take for you to learn to trust Him?

Moment of thought and reflection: What does trust mean to you and why is it so significant to your healing.

*Keep these notes for your own reflection and discuss with your support circle

Can I really let go?

I know you wonder what you would do if you actually let go of the abuse. In other words, get out of your comfort zone. Yes, I said comfort zone. Believe it or not after walking around for so long with the all the feelings of abuse that you have received you get comfortable with it; it fits like an old shoe; it is like the pair of jeans or shorts you love to wear around the house. I never thought about it until one day it was brought to my attention that I was still carrying around the abuse. The thought made me realize that I didn't know who I was without the feelings associated with abuse. I had been dealing with it for so long that I wasn't sure what my life would be without all those feelings, I was afraid. Afraid of what I would think and feel without my familiar feelings, I was so used to them that for them to be gone made me nervous. I had no identity outside of an abuse victim. Every waking moment I was a victim, I wore abuse like a badge of honor. It was my constant companion and, at times, my only friend. I was comfortable knowing that I was a victim. The pain and hurt associated with that victimhood was something that I was accustomed to I had no identity outside of the abuse.

You put on a mask, a mask that says either I am always happy, or no one can ever see the side of me that is pain and in turmoil, or it can be a mask that says you are very rude and always like to be alone, that you are thrilled when people always ask you why you are so mean or why are you always frowning? For me, I was so used to waking up every morning putting on that mask, the one where I always had a frown on my face I never smiled. I was a loner. I had no friends. I didn't want anyone close to me, not even my mother, whom I lived with. I had a wall up, I needed to keep people away from my heart. When someone has been abused, they learn, or at least I did at an early age, to not let what I was really dealing with show. Does this sound familiar? "What goes on in this house stays in this house". this was a sentiment that was ingrained in me from a young age. For years, I was afraid to tell anyone about the abuse. I knew that my family was prominent in the community and looked up to so anything that I said would be considered detrimental to my family. After all, they were in ministry and who would want to believe that their Pastor, Deacon, evangelist would harm any of their children.

From those experiences, I learned to put on a mask and wore one every day for the next twenty years. Yes, over twenty years I wore the mask of anger and constantly had a look on my face that was specifically designed for one purpose to keep people away from me. I felt that if you could not get to me, then you could not hurt me. This was a coping mechanism for me. What is a coping mechanism? A coping mechanism is defined as the plan of action an individual reverts to when dealing with trauma or stressful situations to help the handle painful or difficult emotions. What does that really mean? It means that as an individual grows, and their experiences change the strategies that they use to deal with those situations are developed. It is important to note that there are several factors that affect a person's ability to cope, especially in children. If a child is introduced to a traumatic situation and are engulfed in that situation for an extended period, this can affect how the child learns to cope and often the mechanism used are themselves in a lot of ways ineffective because the child does not have the mental maturity and development to employ adequate strategies to help them deal with the situation. To understand the coping mechanism that you may be using and to understand whether those skills are effective is the first step in removing the masks that we wear. We will learn to take off these masks. Some of us may wear more than one, so we will take them off layer by layer, this cannot be done without the help and support of Jesus and the help of others, those who have overcome. For some intense psychological therapy, medication, and counseling may also be necessary.

A distinctive method of characterizing coping tactics is the **BASIC Ph Coping Model** established by Dr. Mooli Lahad, Director of the Community Stress Prevention Center in Qiryat Shmona, Israel. This modality implies that individuals retain six prospective attributes or factors which make up the foundation of a person's surviving design. Each person has the intrinsic capability to employ every component as a portion of their methodology with regard to coping, even though, generally individuals tend to depend upon easy coping techniques they have established across and extended period. Managing attempts are believed to be efficient, provided a young person can maintain his or her fundamental practice. Parental figures in conjunction with educators can support youngsters in increasing their surviving range by offering the setting, shaping, and support essential to assist, reinforce and create innovative competences. (*How children cope with ongoing threat and trauma: The BASIC Ph Model, Frank Zenere, E. Ds., Crisis Management Specialist for Miami-Dade Public Schools and a former member of NASP's National Emergency Assistance Team.* www.nasponline.org)

First, let's look at coping styles. There are six different ways that children deal with abuse and these can follow into adulthood. They are defined as follows:

- Belief-this is defined as the core values of the individual so for a child or person who deals with trauma or has dealt with trauma one of the first ways that we learn to cope is based on our belief system.
- Affect-this strategy is strictly emotional, often those who deal with trauma, especially in early childhood tries and deal with the issue from an emotional standpoint, it is how person feels emotionally and often is woefully inadequate for most situations, especially when dealing with trauma. The reason for this is since trauma is so impactful mentally, physically, and emotionally acting out of those emotions can lead to other issues with coping with stress or painful issues.

- Socially The core of this strategy is designed around how a person deals with stressful or traumatic situations by relying on others to help them to understand and gauge how to properly deal with a situation.
- Imagination-this is the ability to use their creativity to deal with the trauma or stressful situation. For instance, when dealing with children who have been abused, they are often asked to draw or paint how they feel. This is a way for the child to express how they feel about the situation through a creative means. Of ten children who have been abused will draw themselves and how they feel by utilizing colors to properly convey their inner feelings. (For instance, a child my drawn themselves inside a home with flames or blood or even with the color black to signify how they feel inside.
- Cognitive-This means that there are some children who can understand what they are feeling and work through those feelings intellectually approaching the issue
  from a cognitive approach lets them take the clinical observations and understanding of
  the situation based on their level of cognitive maturity and ability.
- Physiological- this approach is used by some children and adults who are experiencing or have experienced trauma. They will often find a physical activity such as jogging or weightlifting or some other physical activity. This diverts their attention from the issue that is stressing them, allowing them to properly cope with the situation.

Knowing what the ways to cope opens you up to understand how you have been dealing with the trauma in your life and can help you see the masks that you wear. So, what is masking? Masking is often defined as concealing one's emotions by exhibiting an alternate emotion for the situation. To understand the masks that we wear and how to remove them, we must first learn what masks are. First masking is often done without the individual even consciously knowing that they are doing it. The hard truth is that masking is generally covering up one's authentic personality, which the person fears are undesirable to society. The person fears that the way they feel authentically will not be accepted by those around them, so, for instance, we smile even when we are sad. We can be angry about the abuse that we suffered or are dealing with, but will cover or mask that emotion by being overly friendly and showing the opposite of the anger that we feel. There is also the mask that I wore for several years I showed the mask of a discerning and Strick individual. I was not approachable by choice and design, so the mask that I wore was specifically designed to keep others away from me and not give them access to my genuine feelings or emotions about any situation.

Here are some examples of different masks:

- The mask of perfection- This is the persona of a person whose life could be in chaos and ruin, but the mask that they show is that of someone who has it all together their life is ideally perfect. There are no issues or anything that is out of order or place.
- The mask of the comedian-This is the persona is the jokester of the group they find a way to turn everything into a joke or comedy they will often make themselves the butt of the joke. This shows that they are ideally ok with their current situation and though truly they are hurt on the inside, they only allow the smiling funny comedic side to show.
- The intellectual mask-This is the persona who has an extensive vocabulary and they are often full of little-known facts about various subjects this person often speaks in absolutes and always seems to know the correct or acceptable academic or intellectual answer to any question or concern
- The superhero mask-This is the persona of always being the person who comes to the aid or rescue or others. This type of mask will show in that the person spends most of their time being the one that others come to when they are having difficulty this person always has the correct advice to give and will help in every way they can anyone who is in need, even to the detriment of their own life.
- The mask of rudeness-This persona comes with the I am who I am, and I am not changing for you or anyone else personality. These individuals are often abrupt in their speech and they are unapologetic about how they approach others, even if they say something that is hurtful to the other person.
- The mask of ignorance- This persona is usually the person who says that they do not know or comprehend what anyone around them is talking about. They are unable or feign the inability to articulate what they are dealing with within a given social structure.

It is essential to know that therefore going through this process takes a team or group effort. You need to begin to surround yourself with people that you can be authentic with. It is important to surround yourself with those people that God puts in your life to encourage you through this process, those that motivate you to succeed, those who cry when you cry, rejoice when you are happy. Pray you through when things get hard, suffer with you when you are hurting, pray for strength for you when you feel weak. For me, this process was arduous because of the issues I had trusting others and myself. I needed someone who I could be my authentic self with. Through fasting and prayer and constantly asking God for direction. He finally placed someone in my life who was all that I needed to help me take off the many masks that I wore. That person laughed with me, cried with me, encouraged me, and is a constant pillar of support in my life, even to this day.

That person for me became my one truly authentic friend. Friend is not a term I use loosely. I will generally tell people I do not have friends, I have acquaintances. Why did I only have acquaintances? That was part of my mask. I kept people at arm's length. That way, I was not forced to be genuine with them. I could stay superficial. Which was easier for me to maneuver and allowed for the other masks I wore to be used. Until this person came into my life, I was not fully healed because, although I was in counseling and was doing the work. I still had reservations and kept my masks on and my guard up. When this person came into my life, they started by simply saying hello. They left the interaction open ended, they waited for me to make the next move. It took some time because I was cautious, but I found that the more time I spent around this person observing their behavior and mannerisms, that this person was a lot like me. They

themselves had been through some storms in their life. They had experienced some traumas and deep hurts emotionally and physically over the years, but they seemed at peace with their situation and I wanted to know how or why they were at peace, even in the midst of turmoil. I took the first tentative steps by starting a superficial conversation one day I found that talking to this person was easy. It was not forced or rushed. I was assured on every hand by their demeanor and relatability. That person has, over time, become one of my biggest supporters and is a pivotal reason this book is now in your hands. Through this person, I could finally peel back the layers of my life and the masks that I wore to cover what I was truly feeling. One day as we sat on the beach staring at the water, they said to me, "do you realize how beautiful you are as a person? You are such a caring, kind, and wonderful person and it is my privilege to be here with you, helping you be all that you can be, helping you accomplish all that you want to accomplish in this life". That was the first time in my adult life that someone encouraged me wanted to know me the real me, not the masked persona I wore, but wanted to know me Lesa the person. They were not interested in my title in ministry, how many degrees I held, who I knew in a position of power or influence. They didn't want to use me and be around me just for what I could do for them. They wanted to know me, the little girl that tried so hard to show that she was a capable and formidable woman That was when the first mask came off. The mask of perfection I worked so hard at portraying the perfect person that it was refreshing to be around someone who wanted to see me as flawed and imperfect. They validated it was ok not to be perfect that it was not a bad thing to let some of my imperfections show they didn't walk away the first time I stumbled. They stayed.

I see Jesus loved me enough to send someone into my life that can be there with me through my trials and I know everything will work out. Not only did I now have a friend that I knew I could lean on God also blessed me with a Spiritual mother that took me under her wing. From this powerful woman of God, I was able to learn how to operate in the gifts and calling that is on my life. I have over the years been in every facet of ministry, but never was I more keenly aware of what God needed of me than with this mighty Woman of God. My love for her and my friend has only increased over the years. The one thing that I have learned and understood more than anything else, you cannot survive or thrive in this world without having someone there to support and encourage you. No man is an island unto himself was something my grandmother would say to me as a child. The same is true when healing from the hurts that you have faced in this life. This is not a walk that you should walk alone. trust me, I tried for years to walk this one out by myself however, I never reached a place of complete healing and deliverance until I could trust someone other than myself and God.

Know this: God always gives you people who will help you through, but you have to trust him and reach out to those that he tells you to. A word of caution: I have found on this journey you will run into people who cannot handle the abuse that you have gone through. They cannot see past it. Every time they look at you, they are only looking at the abuse survivor. They do not see the overcomer. Those are the people that you should avoid. therefore, I say you must consult God and trust him to lead you. It is imperative that you rely on God and your own instincts with who you release all that you have gone through. It is my firm belief that everyone needs a confidant. What is a confidant, and why are they so vital to this process? The word confidant is defined as someone who is willing to listen to you, no matter what? A personal confidant is a person who is fully engaged and acknowledges and validates your feelings with words of encouragement, they are compassionate. They deliver candid and reliable feedback to the person confiding in them. They are gentle and deliberate in their actions towards you and approach things with an open heart, and an eagerness to facilitate change in the life of another without being derogatory or judgmental or adding their personal opinions or assigning blame to the individual they are dealing with.

What does that really mean? It means especially in the instances of abuse whether in the past or the person is still active in an abusive situation they need someone who will listen and take the actions needed to make sure that person feels safe and protected knowing that what they speak to them about will go no further unless it is in an effort to help them get out of an actively abusive situation. Even in that regard, the confidant understands that if they need to release sensitive information in order to help the individual, they will do it in such a way that the victim of the abuse is not negatively impacted by their assistance and intervention.

There were a few times I didn't seek Jesus about a person and those people ended up hurting me more which made me want to give up, but Jesus stepped in and sent me two very special ladies to help me complete this journey, just as he sent them to me, he will send them to you. You can make it beyond this point. Trust this process. Trust God to put the right people around you and if you do not have any family or friends, so to speak of then seek support groups in your area don't do this by yourself.

With the Christian faith and social structure there are several ways that we cope which can lead to different outcomes however the most positive research shows that when someone has a confidant who they are able to share their most intimate thoughts to the person does not experience as much depression and anxiety that is often associated with recovery from Trauma. (Gall, 2006). Spiritual discontentment or anger with God about the abuse is often correlated with elevated levels of depression, contrary to that when an individual surrounds themselves with a positive individual or group such as a support group for survivors then the rate at which that person can come to grips with the aftereffects of the trauma is decreased allowing the person to begin the delicate process of healing in a shorter time frame (Walsh et al.).

Understanding this shows the importance of having the right people around you or in your circle. How do I choose the right person as a confidant? Look at your current circle of friends or people that you are associated with and evaluate whether they have the right characteristics to be a confidant to you. A true confidant has specific characteristics that you should look for. If they do not have those qualities, then they are not a suitable confidant. The characteristics of a confidant are:

- Active listener- this is someone who makes sure that you feel heard they do not offer unsolicited advice and never steer the conversation in the direction of their own personal problems. They stay completely engaged and show a willingness to give credence to the hurt and pain that you are dealing with.
- Empathetic-They can actually put themselves in your shoes. Not only can they sympathize but they can embody and step into your shoes, giving true validation to your feelings by understanding and internalizing your pain with no negative effects.
- Trustworthy-Here is the word trust again. The person you choose as a confidant must be trusted you are releasing some very personal and serious information you must trust and know that the information given goes no further than your confidant.
- Nonjudgmental- The person you choose as a confidant will display this characteristic in all that they do as it relates to you. They will not look at you like it was your fault or you could have or should have done things differently. When you speak with this individual, they show no judgement they are simply there actively listening and empathizing with you, not judging you.
- Authentic-The person you choose as a confidant will always show you their truly authentic self, they will exhibit a level of vulnerability to you. They will be themselves around you, lending to the fact that they trust you enough to release some of their own fears and anxieties to you letting you truly see them. This, in turn, lets you know that you can trust them because they have no pretenses with you,
- Self-aware- The person you choose as a confidant is consciously aware of their own motives and flaws. They are aware that they have a vital role to play in your healing and recovery and embrace the opportunity to do so.
- Calm- The person you choose as a confidant will have a calm demeanor. There are some hard and heavy times ahead, so you will need someone who will not

panic when you are having a flashback or a painful memory surface. The confidant is always calm and even-tempered as you work through the pain and hurt from the abuse.

- Perceptive- A good confidant is one who can objectively assess a situation without the emotions tied to it, they can see alternatives from a perceptive point of view and offer different solutions to the problem or situation from that viewpoint to give you authentic advice about the given situation.

- Patient- A true confidant is one who does not rush you in any way they understand that the information you are releasing to them is painful and often is extremely sensitive in nature therefore they do not rush you to speak or get past what you are feeling they are always there waiting for you to work through the issues without rushing you to do so.

- Optimistic-With all that, you will release to this person about the pain of your experience, you will need someone who has the glass half full perspective because we often have the other more pessimistic view we expect the worst thing to happen we need someone with the counter to that who believes that there is a healthy plausible solution to the issue at hand and looks for the opportunity to give positive alternatives to the issue looking at it like a problem or issue that will be resolved versus this is a problem or issue that will never be resolved. (Live bold and bloom.com, Barrie Davenport, 2016).

Examine those in your circle to see if they fit these characteristics as a confidant. To narrow it down. ask yourself, is this person empathetic, loyal, calm, trustworthy? Do they give positive, viable advice to situations are they nonjudgmental and do they take the time to listen to you actively, and are they showing you their authentic self? If these are not present, then that person or persons would not be the ideal candidate for a confidant. Remember, you have started a very long and sometimes painfully hard journey emotionally, so you are going to need someone who is willing to go the distance with you and be there through all the ups and downs that this journey will take you through.

Questions:

1. Are there people in your life that you need to stay away from?
2. Do you have a good support system?
3. Can you trust God to lead you to the right people?.

4. Pray and ask God to please help you find the person or persons that can help you through this process.

Moment of thought and reflection: Do you know how to find an excellent support system and what do you think you will open up to them about what you need?
  *keep these notes for your own reflection and discuss with your support circle

Eradicate the past

The discussion has centered on trust and having a confidant and the effects that trauma has on the body, mind, and soul, so now what? How do I shed the layers and lay all of this on Jesus? The question becomes, do I trust him enough to take away the pain and erase your past, enlighten your presence, and excite your future? How do you let go, you may ask? Why is it necessary for me to let go? It is important to shed the layers created by the trauma you experienced. Trauma never really goes away. Often the signs become buried and more subtle. Because trauma, especially childhood sexual trauma, creates a hole in the victims' emotional and mental being that will always be there; does that mean that you will never heal? Please do not despair. Just because trauma has created a hole in your being doesn't mean that you will always feel broken and hurting for the rest of your life.

It means that learning great ways to access these emotions and learning how to cope with the memories is necessary to overcome them. Keep in mind that peeling back these layers of emotions from trauma can take a lifetime to process, but ignoring them will not make them go away. There are several healthy ways to begin the process, but please remember that these are simply examples and suggestions. This is a personal walk, and you need to find the right pattern that works for you. Remember that each person processes trauma differently, so how you heal from that trauma is just as unique and you are.

There is no one size fits all method that will make things better. Everything that you have read so far has led to this moment now that you have learned what trauma is and how it affects you; and that you need to have a support system and learn to trust God. You can now learn how to put this all together. You will need to start with not only surrounding yourself with a great support system even if you just start like I did with one person and God. First, establish a support system. You can create a place that is sacred and safe for your emotional healing. This process will take you through every spectrum of emotion anger, rage, fear, frustration, sadness, pain, grief, bewilderment, and many others.

Because this process can be very traumatic within itself. if you do not have a safe support system, you will need to make sure that you find a stable and healthy person or group of individuals as that support system in place. One of the first things to do is establish a specific dedicated safe space within your home where you can go to release. Dedicating a room or even, in my case, my literal closet. For me, my walk-in closet was the place that I dedicated as a consecrated safe space. I learned early in this process that my closet was perfect for those times when I really wanted to pour my heart out to God. In every home I have lived in since this process began for me, I make sure that there is a closet with a door that can lock on it. Why the closet? For me, it was one of the few places in my home that was quiet. when I was at my lowest and crying out to

God for direction and help, I knew I could get loud, and I did not want my children to hear me and be frightened. When I entered, my closet closed the door. I found that the sound did not travel as much and with the door being locked and the door to my room being locked; I felt more secure. Feeling secure allowed me to relax enough to release all that I held pint up inside.

Once you have an established a safe space, the next things that you must do is stay in touch with your feelings. What do I mean? Every emotion that you have is genuine and there for a reason. Most people who have gone through trauma usually have issues with dealing with their emotions. For me, I found that peace and senility in writing. I would sit down and write about what I had gone through in poetry or in song or just journaling this enabled me to get my feelings out about what I had gone through. I sometimes went for long walks and cried, or I would go into my prayer closet and lay before God and cry. I would tell him about the hurt and the shame and the guilt and the pain. This helped me to get it out.

The earlier in the person's life the trauma occurs, the more difficulty they have processing emotions. I would often find myself in a state of anxiety, especially in new and unfamiliar situations or large crowds of people. Also, I would find myself in moments of such intense deep depression that getting out of bed seemed to be too much effort. I would often neglect even the simplest of things for myself, such as eating or even, at some points, getting out of bed to simply take a shower. At first my mood would cycle between just not caring about anything, to being sensitive to everything. I went through prolonged periods of anger and rage, then guilt because I was angry or frustrated. I did not allow others to see me cry or show that type of emotion as I found in my childhood that crying was looked at as a sign of weakness and weakness makes you vulnerable and vulnerability was a luxury that I did not have.

As a result, accessing my emotions as an adult was very difficult, as I felt that same level of vulnerability and sometimes more intensely, so I found what worked for me to deal with and understand my emotions. I needed to write them down. It took years before I could be venerable with anyone and even to this day there are very few people who are privy to me crying or showing any type of deep hurt. It is something I still work on every day to get in touch with and stay connected to my emotions. I have found that accessing those emotions and having someone to talk to or writing them down allows me to better process them. I found this an arduous task in dealing with the Universal church and how most religious people I encountered approached the subject of mental health.

Previously, we discussed the effects of trauma on the mind and the body from a clinical perspective. I wanted to establish early in this book that there is a difference between what is happening medically and clinically in your mind and body and what is spiritual. I am a firm believer that the body of Christ often speaks in terms of spiritual understanding and disregards the true clinical issues that some people deal with. This was one of the hardest things for me to get around when I started this process.

As well intentioned as they were earlier in my walk with The Father, I had a lot of spiritual leaders that attributed the trauma that I was dealing with and reacting to as being demonically possessed. Sometimes, after I first started in ministry, I felt even more hurt and shame from unlearned leaders who were quick to call what I was dealing with demonic and telling me I was possessed, and that it was a generational curse. While I have since come to realize that unfortunately, when it comes down to mental health, the universal church is lacking in understanding. It does not mean that they are not equipped to handle some of the minor issues that we deal with however it means that sometimes a person is dealing with a serious mental issue, and they are often labeled incorrectly as being demonic or possessed when in reality they are dealing with trauma or some other serious mental health issue.

When someone who is religious and has a specific spiritual view deals with trauma or any of the issues associated with that trauma, such as depression, anxiety, PTSD, etc. Their beliefs and what they have been taught from the Universal church stand-point have to contend with first accepting that they need the help and then complying with a specific treatment plan. This holds true not just for physical ailments, but especially for psychotherapy. Often these patients stay away from what is considered secular treatment options because they often feel as though psychotherapy is not sympathetic to their religious belief system, as well as some feel that seeking mental health help is like abandoning their faith in combination with the feelings of guilt and shame about having a mental health issue. (Koenig H. G. (2012). Religious versus Conventional Psychotherapy for Major Depression in Patients with Chronic Medical Illness: Rationale, Methods, and Preliminary Results.).

For me, this was a battle, especially because of the family that I grew up with. I struggled with mental health and needing help for years, but my family looked at it as a betrayal to the church and to them. From the paternal side of my family, who are all Pastors, Deacon, Evangelist, Sunday school teachers, having issues with mental health was an attack on their character, after all the pastor's daughter could not be seen going to a therapist for any reason. There was also the issue with if I spoke to a therapist and told them what I was really dealing with, then my family would be shammed and that was unacceptable. They had an image that they wanted to make sure was kept intact, in other words as they would often say (What goes on in this house stays in this house and strangers are never to know).

I know I am not the only one who has heard those words, but because I did, I found I was afraid to talk to anyone about the issue. As a result, at thirteen, I attempted suicide for the first time. As you can see, I failed. However, the impact that my mental health had on my life and not having anyone willing to allow me to get professional help was devastating for years. From the maternal side of my family, I had a very similar experience with one big difference and that difference was my mother, a formidable woman who was and is extremely religious and not in the best of ways. She found the concept of therapy to be a betrayal to God and thus discouraged me from getting help for years. She even, at one point, went so far as to sabotage my treatment by going to my psychologist and therapist and telling them I was lying to them. It was difficult to have my doctor and therapist inform me they felt that my mother was a hinderance to my mental health and I should not be around her. Especially when she was the only family I had.

I recall her telling me often that if I had the "right" type of relationship with God, then I would not need therapy. From her viewpoint, my faith was not strong enough and as a result, I was weak mentally for needing help. I was told to give it all over to God and He will fix it and since He had not fixed it, that meant that I didn't have the faith required to get the relief I needed from God. This could not be further from the truth. My faith in God is the one constant in my life. I know God to be a healer. He has healed me several times when the doctors said that I should be dead. God healed me. God healed me when I couldn't walk because of health issues. When I needed lifesaving surgery and the doctors told my mother that I may never wake up from the coma I was in, God healed me. When battling cancer, God healed me. So, faith was not the issue.

The issue was that they had given me a deliberately manufactured lie that if you have depression, anxiety, major depression, Bi-polar disorder etc then you are possessed because those types of things to not affect those who are true children of God. That could not have been further from the truth, but because I grew up in a strictly religious environment, the stigma of having any type of mental health issue was taboo.

The devastating impact that this type of thought process had on me was astronomical I spent years asking God to remove the burden of depression and to heal me from the effects of the trauma I suffered, and years telling myself that God allowed what happened to me to test my faith in Him. Every time I would fall into depression, I would pray in earnest that God would take it away and when I was not instantly granted peace of mind, it shook my faith in Him. Because of misinformation and selfishness on my family's part, not wanting the world to know that they were abusive, I suffered, while my belief in God has changed. Now my walk with Him is for the better. I no longer look at God as a tyrant who doesn't love me. He is my Father truly and for that relationship, I will be forever grateful.

When I stopped looking at God through overly religious eyes and started seeking a genuine relationship with Him, He taught me that there is nothing wrong with seeking professional help for mental health whether it be from a secular counselor or one with a Religious or theological background. He taught me He made physicians for a reason. After all, Luke, the disciple who walked with Jesus, was a physician. While the Bible does not specify what type of physician the fact that he was a doctor should let people know and understand that God has no issues with physicians of any kind or sort.

I understand as well that there are some who are a part of our African American culture that have an instilled mistrust of anyone in the medical profession because of the issues we have faced as a race and culture in this country. Although that is disheartening, is helps others to understand why seeking treatment for any type of ailment in the African American community, especially for our elderly, as they still remember some of the horrors that our culture has experienced. For the African American community, the rate at which treatment for medical issues is sought is significantly less than for those from other races. This comes from experimentation that was performed on African Americans, such as the Tuskegee syphilis experiment. From a therapeutic or psychological point of view, the atrocities that African Americans faced was even worse. For this and other reasons, African Americans are more distrusting of physicians and therapist especially.

In the Native American culture, this is also an issue for some of the same reasons. In both cultures of which I am proud to be a part of we find that the subject of mental health and trauma has been in the past discouraged however as we evolve and grow in our understanding, we now know that struggling with issues of trauma and other mental health concerns is something that can no longer be hidden or unspoken. We must break down the old barriers and mindsets to help those within our community and others to understand the value of good mental health as it related to their spirituality, there by breaking down the stereotypes associated with seeking medical treatment of any kind.

To shed the layers, you must first understand that trauma causes a wound that is not always seen as a physical scar, but an emotional one. For instance, a person who has been in a serious accident or fire carries physical scars related to that event that can be a constant reminder of the event itself, while on the other side, emotional trauma such as the kind people who have faced abuse in their past or childhood and even their adulthood develop scars that cannot be seen with the naked eye, yet they are still scars. It is imperative that you understand and work through those emotions for your complete healing. There are several series of articles and techniques that you can use to begin to heal those types of traumas these are called Trauma Releasing exercises or (TRE).

Why do we need to release emotional trauma? The answer is simple when traumatic events occur. The energy from those events becomes stored in the body and can manifest in many different ways. For me, before I began this process, I dealt with a lot of body aches, headaches, fatigue, nausea, and a host of other symptoms at first. I thought that there was something wrong with me physically, so off to the doctor I went.

This was twofold in that going to the doctor with various symptoms and issues causes the doctor to do a myriad of tests. We were able to ascertain that indeed I had a medical condition an autoimmune disease known as Lupus, as well as Rheumatoid Arthritis. This was diagnosed in my early twenties. Once the doctor got me on a working regimen of medication for the lupus, I assumed that some of the physical symptoms would go away, however that was not the case. Not only did I have physical pain, but there were also times that I would experience full body flashbacks. Something that I smelled or saw would trigger a memory and instantly I would be transported in a sense back to the event or point of trauma. I was not physically there, but my mind and body reacted as if I was there. For years I fought these flashbacks but was unsure how to combat them or even why I was still dealing with them. To shed the layers, I first needed to understand what was happening to me.

First, what is a flashback from the American Psychological Association defines flashback as the following.

1. the reliving of a traumatic event after at least some initial adjustment to the trauma appears to have been made. Memories may be triggered by words, sounds, smells, or scenes that are reminiscent of the original trauma (as in a backfiring car triggering a flashback to being in combat). Flashbacks may be associated with posttraumatic stress disorder.

2. the spontaneous recurrence of the perceptual distortions and disorientation to time and place experienced during a previous period of hallucinogen intoxication. Flashbacks may occur months or even years after the last use of the drug and are associated particularly with LSD. (APA.org, 2021).

In layman's terms, what that means is that a flashback is essentially the individual is reliving the traumatic event as if was being experienced for the first time. Flashbacks are something that people who have experienced CPTSD or Complex Post Traumatic Stress Disorder deal with often, sometimes daily. What is CPTSD? CPTSD results from chronic long-term traumatization lasting months or years, specifically when that trauma happens during childhood. The types of abuse can include emotional, physical, sexual abuse, human trafficking, living in a combat zone, living with unusually high instances of violence such as gun violence, just to name a few. When these events happen in childhood when the individual's brain is still developing, and the child does not have the cognitive function necessary to combat the stress the child often develops CPTSD. (Palic, S., Zerach, G., Shevlin, M., Zeligman, Z., Elklit, A., & Solomon, Z. (2016)) For me because I spent my early childhood and well into some of my adulthood being victimized, I experienced multiple times sexual abuse, incest, rape, beatings, torture, and even being burned in one of the most intimate areas of my body. The repeated trauma experienced from those and other events like it led to me developing CPTSD. What did that mean in the long term for me? It meant that for years I suffered from repeated flashbacks of those trauma's, they would be triggered by different means either a smell, a particular feeling, the appearance of certain individuals would take me back to a place of torment because they looked like the people who harmed me? I had trouble adjusting in certain situations and would often stay to myself because of the flashbacks, since experiencing them sometimes was frightening for others to witness. I would get hot all over, my heart would race, I would become rigid and tense, I would experience intense pain in my stomach. Often, even my intimate areas would hurt. I would feel as though I was being raped or beaten all over again. For me, the flashbacks were even harder to deal with than the initial trauma sometimes because I could not differentiate in my mind the actual event from the flashback to the same event.

There are ways to combat flashbacks and I implore you to try some of them or even research for more understanding to work through your personal battles with memories or flashbacks. Some methods include:

- First understand your triggers-figure out what triggers or activates your flashback is it a sound, smell, taste, or even a specific color or phrase that you may hear.
- Talk yourself down-when you start to experience a flashback, tell yourself ok you are not in the place where the trauma occurred. You are not back there, you are here and in this present time, this is what you are doing. In other words, begin to ground yourself in the present.
- Take long, deep, cleansing breaths. Most people do not understand the significance and importance of breathing. The reason for taking those deep breaths is twofold number 1. It distracts you from the flashback and second taking deep breaths slows your heart rate, lowers your blood pressure, and can lower the level of stress you are experiencing all things that are heightened and elevated when you are having a flashback.
- Sooth your senses- Use sights around you or soothing sounds when I would deal with seizures. My friend would say to me to focus on my breathing, they would divert my focus from the seizure to them, therefore altering the effects of the event, so begin to refocus, use music or colors or patterns or shapes that calm your senses.
- Do not self-harm or be upset with yourself- If you cannot use these and other methods effectively at first do not beat yourself up. Don't fall into the pattern of being angry that you experienced a full flashback or panic Attack or heightened anxiety. We learn at an early age to blame ourselves. It must be something we did or said that caused the trauma to happen. (De Jongh, A., Resick, P. A., I. A. (2016).

Beating yourself up feeds into that same pattern. Trust me, you will not get it right every time and when you cannot combat the flashback, do not disparage yourself or talk down to yourself, essentially tearing down your own growth and success. Last, consider some outside intervention, such as therapy. As I have said to you before in this book, I am a big advocate. If you need therapy, then please seek a credible, reliable therapist. Some of the trauma or issues you may have faced may require the intervention of a therapist to help retrain your cognitive function, leading you to a healthy psychological state of mind. In order to shed the layers of the pain that I was holding, I had to first understand what was happening to me. In order to learn about what was happening to me I went to school I pursued an education in mental health counseling.

The overall goal was not just to be a therapist, but rather to understand why I was experiencing the things that I was and how could I combat what I was feeling.

After studying Pastoral Counseling, I had some understanding but not to the degree that I wanted, so I pursued a master's degree in clinical mental health counseling. Although I have the formal education, I am not writing this book from the clinical standpoint, I am writing it just to help others understand what they are experiencing and how my journey may help them overcome. The knowledge gained from school helped me to map a way out of the pit that I felt I would stay in. I needed to understand the issue so that I could map a workable solution that would facilitate the positive response I needed and wanted the end goal to heal and be whole.

The first step after gaining the knowledge was forgiveness. I started by forgiving myself.

When I say forgive yourself, I mean just this with me. I was angry with myself and my body. I was upset with myself because I felt I should have told more people about the abuse I thought so many times over and over. If I had just told more people, then I would not have been in the nightmare I lived in. I remember once telling a guidance counselor that there was something going on in my home the next day she was gone, but then I also remember when I first went to the school in the next city for pregnant girls. I wanted to tell the teachers there that I was being abused, but I was afraid that it would happen again. Fear kept me from reaching out. Then I was mad at myself for being afraid days would go by I would curse at myself I would feel like a failure I was always afraid always wondering what if and for all those reasons and then some I could not forgive myself for a long time. There would be times when I would look at myself in the mirror and say I hate you, you are weak; you are nothing; you are a fool; you deserve what you got. Then, as I began to have a relationship with Jesus, I could only go so far in that relationship because I would always say that how could Jesus love this?

The weakling who could tell no one what she was going through, the little scared girl who was too afraid of her own shadow to run away. One day while I was sitting crying my mother asked me a question, she said Lesa have you forgiven yourself? I thought about it and said forgiven myself for what? When she told me she had to forgive herself for being angry at herself for the abuse she went through. I thought she was nuts, but it kept bothering me. Days, weeks, months, and yes, years went by with me still feeling the same way to the point of me not wanting to live anymore. Unfortunately for me, I again during that time attempted to take my own life, this time with lasting results. That affected me mentally, physically, and especially emotionally. Let me be clear at the time I tried to take my own life. I was operating in ministry. I was a newly ordained minister and spiritually I was making some strides, however; I was still hurting and broken. Here I was preaching and teaching others. They could lean on God for everything, teaching them the same lessons that I grew up being taught from the organization that we were affiliated with. Unfortunately, the doctrine that I grew up in and was deeply imbedded in me, so I too approached mental health as something that I needed to handle on my own. Within in the deep roots of that doctrine, I found they described God as rigid and unyielding in how He expected his people to deal with the issues of this life. This is a direct result in my opinion of misinterpreted scripture. Within the religious circles often this is the case we as people are given to interpreting scripture so that it fits the narrative that we want to present, instead of actually allowing God to minister through us not our opinion or interpretation of what he was and is saying about our lives and relationship with Him.

This background is one of the main reasons that I truly believe in a relationship with God over religious ideology. The year was 2004 and after a long day and service that night I was exhausted and ready just to go home and rest but that was not the case, instead after service that night I got into a verbal altercation with my mother and the person who she was involved with right in front of the church.

After a long screaming, cussing, yelling match, the anger that I held at bay boiled over. I recall on that evening and my memory of that night is muddled; however, my mother and I continued the verbal altercation on the way home. After a horrendous verbally abusive assault from her, our altercation became somewhat physical. She struck me and threw chairs and the table across the room. The altercation lasted for only a short time and during that time the person who she was involved with showed up at my home where the verbal sparring match continued between, she and I. Things came to a head and my mother stormed out. I stood, confused and angry. Everything hit me all at once. I was dealing with the pain from my past, the anger at the situation, and hurt at her perceived betrayal. For me at that time, all that I had in my life was God and my mother. I had become so wrapped up in taking care of and protecting her I could not see what she was really doing. I could not see the manipulation. I could not see the damage that she was inflicting by the constant verbal abuse. I would cry for hours, asking God why I was so evil, because she often told me I was evil, and I was not following God correctly.

I stood in a daze, staring at the back door. At that point, something snapped in me. I felt as if all that I had faced just came crashing in on me. I felt like a connection in my brain came loose; it was as if all the air was sucked out of the room. I was hurt, lost, and angry. I swallowed over 900 pills that night. I took everything that I had all the medications that my doctors prescribed, poured them out on the table, and swallowed. God had other plans for me as I lay on the couch to die. If it were not for one of my brothers in Christ, that would have been my last night on this earth. He called the police and the paramedics after speaking with me on the phone. The reason he called was to tell me he was so sorry for how my mother and her companion treated me while at church and to apologize for my pastor who blamed me for the incident saying that as a minister it was responsibility to make sure that I removed the altercation from the church grounds, which was another layer of betrayal to me. When the police and paramedics arrived, I recall my mother coming back to the house. She stood outside the ambulance door as the paramedics told her what I had done. Her words still ring sometimes in my ear, yet at this point they have no power over me. Her words were," so this is what you call being a Woman of God and an adult. You are so evil that just to punish me, you decided to kill yourself. God will never forgive you for this".

As the tears flowed down my face, the paramedic looked at my mother and said how dare you! How could you say something like that? His questions were valid, but I no longer had the energy to care. I just wanted it to end. I wanted the pain to stop. The constant noise in my head was something I wanted to stop. I wanted and needed every memory, flashback, beating, rape, molestation, torment, and torture to go. I couldn't carry it alone anymore. I couldn't feel trapped and broken any more. I felt as though there was no point to living if all I had to look forward to every day was pain, hurt, guilt, shame, remorse, anger, rage, and disgust. These had been my constant companions for so many years that I was accustomed to them, but I hated them at the same time.

Yes, they were familiar. Every day I woke, they were there. They lived rent free in my head. They were always with me. I woke up and put them on every day like a suit of armor. I carried the heavy load that all the pain and abuse left me with. I could no longer handle it. The question you may ask is how was someone who was in ministry this messed up? Isn't God supposed to be a healer? Wasn't he supposed to take those things away? My answer is yes, God is a healer and God has healed me. It is through Him I sit here today, even writing this for not just myself but for others who are struggling with the lasting effects of the pain and trauma inflicted on them. So yes, that was the lowest point I had come to in my life, but even in that God was there and God watched over me and protected me. I was taken to the hospital and while there, slipped into a coma, because they could not get all the medication out of my system before it broke down. My heart stopped. I woke up to someone performing CPR on me and was back out again. I stayed in a coma for three months. During that time, I was told by nurses that there were no visitors, no one sat by my bedside. No one held my hand or talked to me, no one came to encourage me to fight. Not one solitary soul showed their face.

I woke on a Thursday, looked around the room and my heart sank. I was still here, still trapped in this place, this body, this mind, this hole. Even God did not want me I was even more depressed. As I lay on a ventilator, I couldn't speak, but I could cry out to God from my very soul, and I did. Someone called my mother and told her she should be ashamed of herself for not being there. She showed up at the hospital the next day.

She walked into that hospital room looked down at me. Her first words were, I forgive you for hurting me this way. I forgive you for making these people think I am a terrible mother. I forgive you for abandoning me. Finally, the icing on the cake, you promised to take care of me because I am sick and then you choose to try to kill yourself, so you do not have to live up to your promise to always be there to take care of me. Here I was lying in a hospital bed could not talk or breathe on my own, still dealing with what I felt was God's rejection of me and this is what she had to say. At that moment the betrayal was complete or so I thought, she turned and walked out of the room and told the nurse I will not come back up here again she did this to herself and I could not care less what she goes through she hurt me with this and do not call me again. The nurse was watching me. I could tell she was appalled by what my mother said, but it did not matter to me. I was so broken that I felt I deserved everything that she said to me.

It was three weeks before I was off the ventilator the whole time I went in and out of consciousness. Every time I found myself awake, I cried, cried because of shame and guilt, cried because the words of my parents echoed in my head. One day, I found myself awake and not crying. Still, I could not speak, but I could talk to God, so I did. I lay there pouring my heart and soul out to Him, begging Him for peace and relief. Asking Him why I had to be the one to deal with all of this. Every day I spoke to God, every day I cried out to him and every day I asked for change and acceptance of the things of my past and the ability to overcome them. Then one day I woke and went into prayer. I talked with God about forgiveness. I started out by asking him to forgive me for trying to take my own life. Then I asked that He forgive me for not being strong enough to endure the burden. I asked Him to forgive me for hurting my mother and bringing shame to the ministry I was affiliated with. I asked Him to forgive me for being angry with Him. Last, I asked that He help me forgive myself. That moment, that pivotal moment, brought back the words of my mother Lesa have you forgiven yourself. That moment changed my life. The tears were flowing, but I didn't care. I said to myself, Lesa; I forgive you I repeated that phrase over and over and over I cried, I sobbed, I broke down, but when it was done, I felt such a release. I had finally forgiven myself, and then I could forgive the people who hurt me. I could accept that Jesus not only forgave me for my sins, but he loved me enough to wait until I fully understood that He was there for me. Forgiveness I learned a long time ago was not for the person or people who initially caused the harm forgiveness was for me. Once I could forgive myself, forgiving them became easier.

Several things happen when you forgive each one of these things can be subjective. Let's examine what
forgiveness actually does.

- First when you forgive someone, you are forgiving yourself as well that goes back to being angry with yourself because the initial trauma even occurred once you begin to forgive yourself, it is easier to forgive others and vice versa.
- Forgiveness gives you back your power it takes you from being a victim to victorious you stop being the victim. You stop blaming yourself for what that other person did to you instead of staying trapped in anger, resentment, and unforgiveness while that person moves on with their life, you take your power back. by the one act of forgiveness, you then turn the tables you are saying what you did was not ok. I haven't forgotten, but you don't get to hold me as an emotional hostage

any longer I am stronger and wiser and better because of the experience and instead of breaking me, you have only caused me to triumph and overcome.

- Forgiveness sets you free-when you forgive all the things that bind you, the emotions attached to that act, the pain, anger, bitterness, hatred, betrayal that the act caused those things that you hold on to since it seems to be all that you have left end up being an emotional cage or prison that you live in every waking moment of every day. Forgiveness unlocks the cell that is your mind and causes you to learn how to walk in that freedom, understanding that the trauma caused harm, but it did not break me. I am stronger because of it can be one of the most freeing experiences of your life.
- Forgiveness has a profound impact on your health- unforgiveness harbors negative emotions. These have negative energy, and it takes a lot for the human brain to hold on to all the pain and anger that the trauma you experienced produces. It is mentally exhausting and often can lead to a person being physically ill from the stress of holding it all in when you forgive, you get to release all those negative emotions and the stress from those emotions leaves your body, therefore positively impacting your overall physical and psychological health.
- Forgiveness helps you move forward spiritually when you forgive yourself and those who have harmed you, a new dialogue opens between you and God. For me, once I forgave myself, I found that spiritually I was better able to move to a place of forgiveness for those who caused the trauma.

Spiritually, I felt that my relationship with God became deeper and more meaningful. I felt I could communicate with him more authentically and effectively, therefore allowing my spiritual enlightenment to grow and, as I grew spiritually, I grew mentally as well as I moved from victim to victor, my relationship with God became more tangible and a solid foundation which I currently boldly stand, telling others that there is hope after the pain and healing after the trauma and victory after being victimized.

Second, sit down and think about how you react every day. Take the time to document your reactions to unique events that happen to you as the day goes on. Take a journal with you jot down feelings thoughts smell facial expressions. After a while (I would do this about once every two weeks) take one day, sit down and look over the things that you have written, then think about your reactions. Are you always happy when you are in public, or do you have a look that says do not touch me, stay away from me?

Do you hide behind eyeglasses or baggy clothes, do you keep people at a distance even when you consider them your friends, do you curse a lot pick fights with everyone who comes in contact with; or do you not talk at all? Try to look inconspicuous try to blend into your surroundings. Do you try hard to not let people see you? Or are you wearing the mask that makes you act as if you are the happiest person around, were you known as the class clown, the person who is always the life of the party, the one who is always volunteering for every project and program at church or at the office.

Once you figure out which mask you are wearing, pray ask Jesus to peel off the layers that you have been hiding behind for years. Try this exercise go to your mirror any mirror study your reflection start by telling yourself that you forgive yourself, tell yourself that you love you, start saying the name or names of the people who have hurt and abused you with each name declare you forgive them, ask God to help you love them. Yes, you must learn to love them. You cannot get to heaven unless you love everyone. I know that at the moment it may seem like something that you will never do, but you must. Think about it this way the person or persons that abused you took something from you they took your power they did something to you that was against your will and in doing so they took the power away from you to control what happens to your body and your mind so learning to forgive them and yes love them gives you your power back. While you are up at night afraid to go to sleep because you don't want to have another nightmare, or you are taking sleeping pills two or three at a time so you can go to sleep and not dream. The people who hurt you are often laid in their bed comfortable sleeping like babies. So why would you spend the rest of your life miserable and unable to rest because they have put fear and terror in your heart Forgive them not for them but for you, love them not for them but for your healing and deliverance from the pains of your past and the anguish of your memories do this so that you will have a better present and a brighter future. Be willing to take off the mask. If you are always frowning, then stand in the mirror and start smiling practice it every day take twenty minutes in the morning and stand in the mirror and smile keep practicing it every time you feel yourself frowning smile every time you feel anger smile when you are going on about your day every once in a while smile this will help you take the scowl off your face and people will warm up to you. If you are always hyper, tell yourself to stay calm practice it tell yourself during the day while you go about your daily routine stay calm stop when you feel it and count to ten while counting say one Jesus loves me. Two Jesus died for me. Three, I am a child of God. Four Jesus is always there for me. Five, the Holy Spirit is my comforter. Six, I can be calm and rest in knowing Jesus loves me. Seven, Jesus will never leave me, not forsake me. Eight let this mind be in me that is also in Christ Jesus. Nine, God is the sustainer of my life. Ten I can do all things through Christ that strengthens me. Keep doing this throughout your day and do it every day until you notice you are no longer as hyper. Know that you can use whatever encouraging words or phrases you would like the ones above I used when my son had issues with hyperactivity. They were used with therapy and medication. Remember, you do not always have to be the center of attention it is okay for someone else to take the spotlight. If you are trying to fade into the background, reach out to people at work or in the church. Start conversations small ones at first maybe while at work talk to the person next to you start slow try good morning, ask them if they would like a cup of coffee. If you are at church, go up to someone and hug them a genuine hug, not the ones you usually give that say. Leave me alone. I am only doing this because everyone else is. Invite one person out to lunch. Wear brighter colors so that you don't just blend into the background. I know this seems trivial, but I found that just by changing the colors of my clothing, my attitude changed. Instead of wearing everything that was black and dark, I started with a bright yellow shirt. At first, looking in the mirror, I hated it because it was so bright. But all day I got compliments from people. This was a confidence booster to my self-esteem. Say to yourself I am worth loving I am worth having a friendship. I can do this. These examples are things that help me reprogram my mind. When the abuse occurred, you were wired with certain thoughts and those thought governed how you lived your life.

If you were verbally abused like I was, I had to reprogram the thoughts that my dad put in my head. Every time I would hear you will never amount to anything I would say in Jesus I am a new creature, or when I would hear you are crazy like your mother, I would say to myself for God has not given us the spirit of fear but of power and of love and a sound mind. Or when I would hear no one is ever going to love you, I would say to myself, for God so loved the world that he gave his only begotten son. I used scriptures to defeat the enemy. The word of God is power and with that power, you can defeat all that the enemy tries to throw at you. Take up your Bible search for scriptures if you cannot find any I have included some in the back of this book, begin to study those scriptures meditate on them memorize them so when the enemy tries to attack your mind you will have something to fight him with this will allow you to clear your mind and remove some layers of pain that you have been carrying around for so long. For those of you who may say, but I am not a spiritual person. I have no use for God or that you do not believe in God. Understand this above all else. If it were not for God in my life, I would not have made it through all that I have. This book is written from my experience. Everyone may not get saved or have the gift of salvation, but everyone deserves to be healed and whole no matter their race, color, creed or gender. Take the tools that you learn from this book don't disregard them because they are written from the point of view of having a relationship with God. Allow yourself the option and opportunity for healing growth and development. Find other motivational affirmations that are more suited to you. How you feel about God or anything else is not the focus. I understand as there was a time in my life that I willingly walked away from God. That was one of the most difficult and devastating times in my life. I found my way back to Him, and He was still there and still loving on me. You don't have to be religious to be healed you just have to be willing to walk out the process and put in the work needed to facilitate that healing and you may find that this was the plan of God all the time; He loves you enough to make sure that you are healed from the hurt, so accept it and walk in your healing.

Questions:

1. Have you forgiven yourself?
2. Have you forgiven your abuser? Can you learn to love them?
3. What mask are you hiding behind?
4. What steps do you need to take to remove the masks that you wear?

Moment of thought and reflection: Is forgiveness something that you really think is attainable for yourself and how do you plan to go about forgiving yourself
  *keep these notes for your own reflection and discuss with your support circle

Everlasting Peace

What I found while going through all of this was that most of the time, I felt like I was in constant turmoil. Everything I did, everywhere I went; my mind was always on the memories of the past. It kept me awake at night; it kept me irritable during the day. I never wanted to do anything. I was for a long time in a deep depression. From head to toe, I wore black. I wanted nothing to do with life. Sometimes I couldn't focus. The only thing on my mind was the abuse I suffered. The faces of the people who hurt me haunted me day and night.

I did so many things to cover up the pain that I was in. After I woke, I drank until I went to sleep. I engaged in reckless behavior sexually; I turned to a life of illicit as well as prescription drugs. Even though I had been baptized at 12 years old, I was in a back-slidden state. I had turned away from God and I was in no mood to go back. My life was going nowhere, and that was just the way I wanted it. I just wanted to crawl into a hole and die. It didn't matter to me whether I woke up in the morning and often I would be angry when I found myself awake because, to me; it was just another day of misery and pain. I ate myself up to almost 300 pounds and didn't care.

I had no self-esteem and was not invested in my healing or betterment. I had become so accustomed to the trauma that I often created toxic situations so that people would hurt me that way I was right when I said that no one loved me, and no one cared. (Self-fulfilling prophecies) I think, therefore, I am. What I thought about myself; I manifested in all that I did. Because I did not see myself as worthy of love or affection. I dated people who were unaffectionate and unloving. During those relationships, I would often feel useless and like a human garbage can. I have since come to understand that I was projecting the thoughts about myself onto others therefore, essentially; I sabotaged myself daily. Because I thought so little of myself because of the verbal, mental, and emotional trauma that I experienced, I was unable to see the world around me as non-hostile and non-threatening. For me, everyone was not to be trusted and to be kept at arm's length and most definitely no one was to ever see me in what I considered a weak or venerable state.

My walk with Christ has been arduous not because of Him but because of my perception of Him and how I approached my relationship with Him- (Apostle Lesa Hunt)

After meeting my mother, the one thing that she insisted on was that I go to church. I remember telling her these words, I will go with you, but I want nothing to do with your God. My mother prayed and prayed, but because of the issues I had with her and the things that she was doing to me, I held out no hope of my relationship with God. It took quite a while for me to even soften my stance on this issue, so I went to church every Sunday and during the week because she made me go. I was so closed off to the concept of God the Father and all that He stood for because until that moment, God had only been a source of pain for me. The people in my life used God as a weapon wielding the Holy Spirt around as a sword cutting down everyone and everything that did not fit their narrative and interpretation of scripture. This put me at a disadvantage when it came to overcoming the pain of my past. How can God heal and deliver you from something like trauma when you don't trust Him enough to allow Him full access to you? I found that even being in church allowed the small relationship I had with God as a child to grow. Slowly, God changed my heart and my outlook on Him and what a relationship with him meant. I had to come to the realization that the only representation I had of God came from damaged and broken people who used God and the word of God to make excuses for the things that they were doing. This understanding caused a rift in the relationship with God and once I realized that my view of God changed, it became necessary for me to dedicate my life to God and to fully accept Him into my life as savior, redeemer, Lord, and King.

When I fully accepted Jesus the second time, I attended church regularly and things seemed to get better, but I still had trouble sleeping and though I had stopped drinking, I was still smoking cigarettes and whenever I tried to quit, I would get terrible anxiety attacks. I wondered if I could ever sleep through the night or would I spend the rest of my life sleeping during the day. I desperately wanted to be what I knew, or thought was normal and just have one night where I could sleep through the night instead of staying awake all night dealing with the memories of my past constantly playing scenarios over and over in my mind.

Even the things that I dealt with from living with my mother and the constant emotional and mental anguish that I faced from her daily. It took years, but I can now sleep through the night without the night terrors that I used to deal with. That victory was hard won, but it was won with God not fighting against Him. The nightmares and thoughts that constantly raced in my mind kept me in inner turmoil. That turmoil caused me to be at constant war within myself, therefore I had no peace. Without peace I could not rest, without rest I could not function as effectively during my daily life. I made sure that I was in constant motion. That way I would not think, and I could compartmentalize all the things that were bombarding my mind and affecting my spirit. For years I survived on three hours of sleep or less a night. That lack of rest meant that my body never got the chance to reboot, so to speak. Because of the lack of sleep, I started getting sick physically, which also contributed to my lack of peace of mind. I was eventually diagnosed with an autoimmune disease called Systemic Lupus Erythematosus. This was a devastating diagnosis for me, which was just one more thing that I had on my mind.

I talked to Jesus. I remember praying for hope and for God to purge me, then while studying his word, one day I came across this scripture. Peace, I leave with you; my [own] peace I now give and bequeath to you. Not as the world gives, do I give to you. Do not let your heart be troubled, neither let it be afraid. [Stop allowing yourself to be agitated and disturbed; and do not permit yourselves to be fearful and intimidated and cowardly and unsettled.] John 14:27 Amp. That is when I realized I was not at peace. I am talking about the peace that only Jesus can bring, not like peace from the world. I'm talking about inner peace that makes you want to live; makes you want to go into the world and face others.

Peace means the absence of war or other hostilities harmony serenity. That is exactly what Jesus supplies only supernaturally. He makes it so that the war that is in your mind can ease he comes in like a sponge and if you let him, he can calm the storms that you are facing in your mind. This concept, for me, was both intriguing and frightening at the same time. How you may ask the answer is simply this. I was so used to living in constant mental turmoil that I was unsure what life would be like without it. As a child, I taught myself to stay awake and alert on constant vigil night and day when I was at home. It was important that I was always one to two steps ahead of my tormentors for me to do that I was constantly thinking of strategies on how to stay ahead of them and out of their way so that they would and could not harm me. Nighttime was the most important to me because it was the time that my uncle and other men were at home. I needed to always stay awake and alert so that no one would sneak up on me and snatch me out of bed. Then there was the constant threat of my oldest biological brother, though only two years older than me. He was crazy fast and extremely cunning, matching that with his misogynistic, sadistic, and insatiable sexual appetite from a young age made him my greatest threat and my family made us sleep in the same space. When you share a space with someone so vicious, you learn early on to stay on your toes.

There are many benefits to having inner peace physiologically, psychologically, and spiritually. First, you must understand the peace that God is giving is nothing like the world. Human peace is totally predicated on those we are around or associated with The peace of man is based in the natural realm. We as human beings get upset based on circumstances and situation. When we have wars, riots, violence of any kind, natural disasters in various places, this causes us to be disturbed and emotionally impacted, causing a shift in our peace of mind.

Spiritual Peace, the peace that Jesus Christ gives and is referring to in this scripture, is the peace that is Spiritual impacting you on the spiritual level knowing that God will supply all your needs and trusting his word that He will never leave you or forsake you. This gives you that spiritual peace. It is just hard to see when you do not trust God. Let's take a deeper look at peace, or inner peace, as some like to call it. First, understand that the outer is often a reflection of what is going on internally. So, a person like myself who experienced different levels of trauma from an early age was introduced to turmoil and upheaval. The violence that raged inside me, the anger, bitterness, fear, guilt, shame, and everything associated with the memories and thoughts that plagued me daily caused me to be in constant battle and, therefore, I had no peace.

For a long time, I would surprise myself and laugh or smile, then I would feel as though I was unworthy of being happy and that I had no right to laugh or even have lighthearted fun. The result was that I mostly felt guilty about being happy, then angry at myself for being guilty about being happy. You see, I felt I did not have the right to be happy or to laugh. Let's be clear there is a distinction between religion and relation-ship when dealing with the impact of trauma. It is important to note that to have peace like the peace described in the text for the person who has experienced trauma is not that simple to come by. There are certain factors in play as it relates to peace for those who have experienced trauma. Having or getting the peace of God can be hard to do because it requires the critical step of totally trusting God. Total surrender and trust in God is extremely difficult because a person's overall image of God is directly influenced by how we are reared during our formative years, this can cause a person to view God either positively or negatively depending on the circumstances that a person is raised in [Bierman A. The Effects of Childhood Maltreatment on Adult Religiosity and Spirituality: Rejecting God the Father Because of Abusive Fathers? J. Sci. Study Relig. 2005; 44:349–359. Doi: 10.1111/j.1468-5906.2005.00290.]

For those who were raised in a household that is not religious or spiritual in any way with no trauma or abuse of any kind, they are left to make their determination about a higher power or religious practice on their own so their first introduction to God may be approached differently. The person who is left to approach God or any other religious belief as an adult they can formulate an educated uninhibited opinion about God free from any preconceived notions of who or what God is and how He positively or negatively impacts their life. However, in direct contrast to that someone like me, who was raised in a very strict religious home where the notion of God was used to keep me in line and obedient to the will of my abusers. My view, like others who were raised this way, was one that looked at God as negative, and non-loving in any way. Statements like God is full of wrath, judgement, and punishment lead me to feel as though God was not someone or something that I wanted to get to know. Research has shown that those like me who were unfortunate enough to grow up in these types of environments have the most difficult time changing their view of God from negative to positive. This was a necessary step for me to gain inner peace. As I have stated time and time again in this book what or who you choose to believe in is totally up to you, for me my relationship with God has been the foundation on which I was able to rebuild my life taking me from a state of self-hatred and self-loathing to a place of self-love and even admiration.

Having God there to lean on and to give all my pain to is what helped me to achieve inner peace. Leaning on His word in conjunction with His will for my life allowed me to share my story with you. Without God and the peace he has provided to me, I could not tell you that though it is dark now, there will be brighter days ahead. Let me be clear: getting to a place of inner peace did not happen for me overnight. I didn't read the scripture quoted above and instantly gain peace. It took some time at first; I fought and argued with myself, then with God. Why did I fight myself? The main reason I fought with myself was because I did not feel as though I had the right to peace of mind. As a child and young adult, I felt like I deserved everything. I felt that what was drilled into me as a child was true; I was nothing. I would never amount to anything. No one could ever love a broken piece of dirt like me. I fought with God because I was angry. How could you offer me peace and let me suffer like you did? How could you give me peace that surpassed my understanding and calmed my heart and mind when you were a tyrant? You allowed these people to hurt and abuse me? If I wasn't important enough for you to protect when I was being abused, how could I be important to you now? How could you want to shield and protect me and give me relief now that I was an adult but did not give a care for me when I needed it the most? This was a constant argument between me and God for quite a few years. Because of my resistance to accepting God, I could not accept the peace that He so freely offered.

As you can see these things build on each other without faith you cannot make it, without trust you cannot have full access to all the benefits that God gives to us, and without Spiritual peace you cannot ever get to the point where the things that you have gone through can no longer cause you psychological pain because you are steadfast in your understanding that God is the ultimate healer and all that you will need to come to peace with the abuse you suffered.

Having peace of mind is one of the best things that could have ever happened to me. I was so down; I was so out of it most of the time I was fighting with so many things even though I was feeling a lot better in Christ, and I was growing by leaps and bounds in ministry, but I would still go home lonely and depressed I would still feel like an outcast. I was still hiding behind the mask, but once I got the revelation that I needed peace and that with peace and a calm mind. I could do more for Christ and I would be able to cope with all the things that happened in my life.

When you are wearing a mask and are not at peace, it often keeps us from taking off the other mask that you are wearing this is because peace is something that happens on the inside it is not a mask that you wear it is a cleansing of the soul. Peace comes in and takes away all the unpleasant places. He fills in the holes that being abused left behind. It is very important that you pray for peace and receive it. Now don't get me wrong, it is difficult there are going to be some challenging times ahead and the peace that comes with the indwelling of the Holy Ghost is invaluable. Peace is so important because it will help you interact with others and, if need be, with the people who abused you. It will help you sleep better at night, and you will enjoy life again for me. It was like weights being lifted just as I felt when I forgave myself and the ones who hurt me. I thank God every day that he gave me his peace. As you have noticed by now, we are going with one goal in mind to be complete.

When I say complete, I mean loving ourselves as well as others, forgiving ourselves as well as others, and embracing Jesus Christ for the peace that he offers and gives to us freely if we only trust him to do so. Peace in the world of an abused person or a person who has abused sometimes is a hard thing to find you get so many mixed signals one minute you're happy the next you are so frustrated that you snap at the first person who speaks to you. This is because your mind is in chaos, your spirit is tired of carrying all that baggage, but your flesh just keeps holding on tight to it. When you get the peace of God that surpasses all understanding, then and only then can the next step be made, but remember peace cannot be achieved without love, forgiveness, and trust in God.

How can you get started on the right path continue to meditate on the scriptures as well as spend quality time in prayer with God not just asking him for anything, but also thank him for all that he has done, ask for forgiveness of your sins, thank him for the things you may have previously requested, then just relax, have a conversation with God. Talk to him about your concerns, confide in him your fears, don't be afraid to show God your tears, worship him for his goodness, worship him for his majesty. Give your heart, mind, body, and soul over to him, ask him to clean you up, confess your sins and when you are finished sit silently for 5 to 10 minutes at first, then when your prayer life gets consistent, the time will lengthen this is a time for reflection and meditation, sitting in the presence of God, basking in his glory waiting for him to tell you what to do, waiting for him to respond to your request, wanting just to be in his presence, reverencing him.

Remember a healthy prayer life, a bountiful study of scripture in conjunction with a steady fruitful helping of the word, strengthens your spirit and your flesh weaker, therefore allowing the peace of God to dwell in you.

Questions:

1. How do you feel most of the time?
2. Are you at peace?
3. Pray and ask God for peace?

Moment of thought and reflection: What can you do personally to obtain Peace? Map out the steps you feel it would take to get you to a place of peace and how would that plan of action be implemented
*keep these notes for your own reflection and discuss with your support circle

Overwhelming Joy

Once you have understood and began to achieve peace, you will find the next step surprising. That step is joy. When you have been abused, no matter what kind of abuse, you tend to lose sight of your joy. Joy given by God is freely done, so you don't have to buy it and you don't have to barter for it. God gives you joy unspeakable. When we look at John 15:10-11 (KJV) It says if ye keep my commandments, ye shall abide in my love; even as I have kept my father's commandments and abide in his love. These things have I spoken unto you, that my joy may remain in you, and that your joy may be full. We see Christ says that if you obey him and love him and abide in him just as he abides in his Father, in him you will have joy. Again, it is all a process you cannot abide in him if you don't first know him, love him, trust him, accept his peace, and then comes the joy that fulfills understanding and love that's where the joy comes in and allows you to continue to heal.

Now understand this happiness and joy are two different things. Joy is an inner knowledge of all the happiness, of the past, present, and future, and the understanding of the ultimate sacrifice that God as Jesus Christ made so that we could live complete lives. Happiness is a human emotion. It is something that we feel outwardly we depend on someone else to give us this emotion or we depend on a memory of a person to bring us this feeling called happiness. Man, on the other hand, does not give Joy. God gives Joy. So, while happiness and inner peace are created by man and are predicated on circumstances and situations.

Joy comes from within. Everyone is born with the capacity to experience and feel true joy. The type that God speaks of joy unspeakable comes from within. When a person has been abused, the ability to feel sustainable, lasting joy often gets blocked or clouded. Though there is plenty of research about the effects of trauma from a clinical stance, I want to approach joy from a more personal point of view. When I look back over my life, there are distinct times that I can truly say I experienced joy. When my two younger children were born, I truly experienced joy. It did not matter that the situation was not ideal or that their father was not with me during their birth bringing them into this world gave me such a sense of joy and in many ways a sense of completion one chapter of my life was over, and a new chapter was beginning. When I first separated from my mother, who was the last of what at the time, I thought was a reminder of the pain and hurt of my past; I felt a sense of Joy. This was not the first thing I felt about that separation. However, it was the result in the end.

Because joy is an emotion that encompasses feelings of contentedness, satisfaction, and harmony, it is not something that depends on an outward source to generate, it is something that must come from within. Well, how do I find or get joy Apostle? Stay encouraged. You do not have to find joy; joy is already here for you and is within you. It is just difficult for you to see and feel right now because you do not know how to access it. When you have gone through pain and grief and trauma for so long, you forget that joy is even possible. For me, it took God reminding me that the joy of the Lord is my strength. I stretched out in that knowledge when I separated from my mother and surrounded myself with people who encouraged and believed in me instead of being around someone who constantly reminded me of my past and the things that she felt I failed in. I sought God for direction and peace of mind during the midnight hours when I lay alone in bed thinking about my life and how much I wanted to do and should have already accomplished. At first, those thoughts made me sad. I felt as if I failed God, my children, and myself. It was God who spoke to me in the dark's quiet; He showed me all that I had accomplished. He brought back all the things that I had been through and said one thing: you made it through Lesa. You made it through no, you may not be where you want to be, but you made it through. Now get up, rediscover the drive that it in you and live.

That motivation made me reexamine my life and where I was and what I wanted to accomplish. I searched within myself and realized that though I have been tested and been through storm after storm, the only thing that could keep me in the place of sorrow, sadness and guilt was me. I needed to replace those emotions with something else, so I started with motivating myself. Every morning I said that it was going to be a great day. I even incorporated this self-motivation into my work life as well. Every day I would put an inspirational quote out to my team. I found that encouraging then also encouraged me, but there was still something missing.

The hard realization was that joy for me came in spurts. I needed to tap into that joy and peace all the time, not just momentarily. This made me want to know more about joy and what it really meant. So again, I researched and came to realize that what I experienced that was momentary was happiness, which is based on emotion what I wanted and needed was joy which comes from within.

So how do you access joy when you are so used to pain and hurt? How do you move beyond the constant day to day of just keeping your head down and not making waves, not calling attention to yourself, and just surviving? You start with not just surviving, but learn to live. Rewrite the old mind maps that you have that tie to your emotions like hurt, pain, anger, resentment, bitterness. These emotions often cloud your thoughts and make joy seem like a fleeting thought for most people who have been through abuse and hurt. Because emotions are easily tangible and can be manipulated by events and people whom we encounter, they are temporary. Joy comes from within; therefore, it is something that is with you continually. It may feel like happiness, but it is different Joy comes from your soul it is one part of the fruit of the spirt. Where do the fruits of the spirt come from? They are birthed from and housed within the Holy Spirit Joy is one of the nine attributes of the Fruit of the Spirit. How then does everyone have joy and can access joy? Everyone can access joy because everyone can house the Holy Spirit once you accept God into your life. Not go to church every Sunday and follow a particular doctrine or dogma, but truly accept God into your life and develop a relationship with Him you allow the Holy Spirit to come in. Having the indwelling of the Holy Spirit brings with you the nine attributes of the Holy Spirt one of which and is one of the most profound is Joy.

So, the question becomes, can I have joy without God? The real genuine answer is no. You can find happiness and contentment with life, but genuine joy only comes from God. Does this mean you have to immediately go out and join a ministry and start operating in some sort of religion? That is not what I said. I said you cannot have joy without God. This means that to have and experience genuine joy, you must have a relationship with God. Where or when you worship or if you ever walk into a sanctuary or edifice of any kind is not indicative of a relationship with God. Those are outward signs to man that you know who God is and that you at least understand Him.

A relationship is unique. It does not require that you walk into an edifice, it does not require you to subscribe to any doctrine or dogma, it simply requires you to establish a dialog and open communication with God. Now will all that comes learning more about Him and for that you will need someone to teach you so you will need to find a true teacher and mentor in the Word of God. In some ways, yes, when you establish a genuine relationship with God, He will direct you to a particular ministry or organization where you can fulfill some essentials of a relationship with Him. It is in a ministry setting where you get your teaching and understanding of the Word of God and your soul gets fed however you must also feed your soul and nurture your relationship with God through daily communication with Him in prayer and reading and studying His word. These things feed your soul, strengthen your spirit, and increase your faith, thereby opening you up to the understanding of what a true joy relationship with Him can bring. Will it happen overnight? Will you learn to trust God instantly? No, it will not and no, you will not trust God instantly. However, building a relationship with Him with realistic expectations will cause genuine change in your life in all areas, especially in experiencing joy.

Through study and my relationship with God, I have found the Joy that for so long I wanted and needed. At first, I wasn't sure that it was joy. I thought I was just experiencing happiness. Then I noticed I would ride down the road singing, not like it used to be when I would sing, when I was depressed or angry to change my mood. But singing just because for no reason. I actively started spending time with my boys going to the beach, something I never did before. I pored over old poems I had written and even found the inspiration within myself to finish this book, which I started over 20 years ago.

It was then I realized my relationship with God and my seeking Him had produced and matured my soul and spirit to the degree that I could see and understand that

I was experiencing not just happiness but true joy that came from within not from the things that were going on around me. Once you find you can access joy and feel the difference between happiness and joy, you will come to understand that there is a profound transformation in your mindset and an understanding of life and the things surrounding you. Instead of always looking at things in the negative, you find you will look to the positive even in situations that are painful and sad you will still be able to see the positive. How it is possible to see the positive and find Joy in sadness? I will use myself as an example. Recently I stepped out on Faith and brought this work and all that I learned to others. I hit roadblock after roadblock but the biggest was financial I knew it would cost to get this work to all who needed it however, I recently ended a relationship and for the first time in my life I was the only person who was bringing an income into my home. We had spent the last two years amid a global pandemic and rent for me was hard to come up with based on my current income. I spent months not eating almost daily to make sure that there was enough food for my children.

Here I was trying to start a publishing company, write a book and take care of my home and children with little to no finances. Yes, I worked every day, but I knew I was 1 paycheck away from being homeless with my kids. There were nights I cried, and fear was constant that I could not provide for them. My car was repossessed eviction notice was on my door and I had no food in the house. The job I work could not cover all my expenses alone and to top it off, they restricted overtime, which was how I was even remotely getting by. At that moment, part of me wanted to give up and say forget it. This can't be done, but something would not let me. I found joy in writing and knowing that what I was getting ready to birth into this earth could help other people dealing with the hurt and pain. My children were watching me go after my dreams and I found joy in that. I found joy in watching the growth and change in my own life as I progressed through the writings that I have held onto for over 22 years. So even amid all the mess that these last few years have brought from the pandemic to racial unrest to confusion about our own health and sanity, I could find things about this process and situation that were joyous. That came not from looking at the outside and all that I was facing. It came from internally and every day I wake up with joy in my heart and a sense of peace and purpose in my life.

Questions?

1. *Have you ever felt genuine joy? If so, when and what context did you experience it?*
2. *Do you think you do not deserve to feel Joy? if so, why or why not?*

Moment of thought and reflection: Write if you feel there is a difference between happiness and joy and how or why it is essential and important in your journey to healing.

*keep these notes for your reflection. Talk about them with your circle and support system.

True Freedom Leads to Growth

What is freedom and in what context are we speaking about? The definition of freedom is the capability or privilege to proceed, declare, or believe as one desires without obstruction or holding back. Now what is freedom as it relates to man, and why do we fight so hard to achieve it? Freedom as it relates to man is often related to and confused with power. While man views freedom as the ability to do as he or she pleases within the letter of the law that is defined by some sort of justice system, it does not really make up freedom. Yes, I can say whatever I want, go where I please, live my daily life with certain rights and liberties that may be, in a sense, physically free, but am I really operating in True Freedom? The answer is, while some are physically free to do all these things and are not confined to some sort of institution or behind prison walls, it does not mean that they are free. What it means is that we can operate in a society that perceives the ability to move about without hinderance and say and do what we choose, is considered freedom, but we are still bound. True Freedom lies in the knowledge and understanding that it is spiritual and signifies recognizing and receiving support from the source that is eternal, which constantly lives, and is everlasting.

How can we navigate a world that is perpetually ruled by our own emotions and really be free without God? The answer: We can't we think we can and in fact we believed we could simply by being given free will. We have the will to choose whether we want to be in a relationship with God or serve Him or not and there by choose spiritual freedom or not. Humans tend to think in the human form. We don't always see the spiritual side of what Jesus (God) says to us. When you were abused, hurt, torn, thrown down, and messed over, you instantly became bound. You became bound by the anger that set in, bound by the hurt that set in, bound by the pain that set in, bound by your emotions. At that moment, you became spiritually locked up and, in a sense, put into a mental and physical prison. Why do I say a physical prison? Often, emotional trauma manifests in the body, causing for some physical pain, inflammation and other health issues related to stress and the stress pain cycle. For me dealing with the memories of my past and having to deal with CPTSD sometimes I would experience intense physical pain in my body. My joints would hurt. I would get stabbing shooting pain in my abdomen and especially in my lower region legs, thighs, hips and back. This pain would cause me to be bedridden for days leading to states of depression and major depressive episodes as a result I felt like I was in a physical prison my body became my cell and the torture that I lived in was a constant reminder of the trauma I endured. These are the things God wants to free you from, these are the situations God wants to take out of you, not let sit and fester, the abuse that you suffered opened a wound in you, and once that wound was opened, it was infected you were infected with all of this pain and problems, then you became bound by sin, Jesus says in John 08:34-37 "I tell you the truth, everyone who sins is a slave to sin." Now a slave has no permanent place in the family, but a son belongs to it forever. So, if the Son (I, Jesus Christ, God) set you free, you will be free indeed.

I know you are Abraham's' descendants; yet you are ready to kill me because you have no room for my word. I am telling you what I have seen in the Fathers' presence and you do what you have heard from your father. What does this mean for you? It means that in God, you come to understand that it is His one desire to make certain that you are free, truly free. Look at trauma and emotional pain like this imagine having to go about your daily activities drive, go pick up the kids, go to the store, to the beach, or just to the park but you have a broken leg, and it is in a cast all the way up to your hip from your foot.

It is there every day, heavy, cumbersome, and always in the way. If you have no help and must be the one to drive yourself everywhere, there is no one to help you get your housework done or to maneuver through your daily duties. Everything you do is impacted by needing to maneuver this thing that is weighing you down and getting in the way. That is the emotional damage induced by the trauma you suffered. It is a constant reminder of the pain that caused the damage. Those emotions always being in a constant state of turmoil, manifesting physically in your life every day, every waking moment. You don't have to imagine it, do you? If you are reading this book, you know exactly what I am talking about. The pain is there, the emotions are there raw and real every day and all you want is to be free of them. So how do I get free? This leads me to my next question: What is the concept of freedom to God and why does He want man to have it? The answer Freedom to God is irrelevant He is God, so He is always free to go anywhere and to do what He chooses because he is the creator of us all He has no need for freedom He is freedom what He desires is that you feel the same sense of being free of your emotional torment and the strain that it puts on you constantly. Emotions are hard for man to control they tend to dictate what we do and can at times cause man to do some very strange and crazy things. God desires to free you from emotional bondage. He desires to teach you emotional control and stability and to, in turn, give you true freedom.

When he frees your spirit, He is seeking to take on the emotional hurt and pain he is seeking to give you peace of mind and help you deal with your emotions in a positive and controlled way so that you can function outside of the chaos of your own mind. For that reason, He gives you the Holy Spirit your comforter. The Holy Spirit filters your emotions and can, if you let it, keep you in a state of calm and peace that keeps your mind free and in a state of constant development and adaptation. Staying emotionally bound often leads to distracted thinking, irrational reactions to minor events that cause our emotions to take over and cause us to respond to perfectly neutral or harmless situations in a radical and unstable way. This leads to those who have been traumatized often traumatizing and victimizing others, whether or not we want to. Because those who have been through trauma do not process emotions the same and are often in a constant state of fight or flight in our minds. We tend to lash out unexpectedly and can inflict serious emotional damage to someone else just trying to navigate in this world. What do I mean by that? Until I was truly free in my mind from the emotional pain that the rape and abuse caused, I would react to what seemed like normal rational situations in an abnormal, irrational way. One example for me was keeping my house clean. Because I grew up in an abusive household, I would often endure physical beatings to the point of sometimes being bloody if I did not clean things how those raising me wanted it cleaned. Everything had a place, and everything must be in the place that it was assigned there could be no dirt on any surface at any time. No dirty dishes in the sink, no soap scum or grime of any kind on any surface. No dust on any surface, nothing out of place. If there was one thing that did not pass the inspection, I was physically beaten, then berated verbally until I corrected what they felt was in error. This led me to be in a constant state of alertness to cleanliness. As the rapes and beating progressed, I had issues with cleanliness. Especially when it came down to after the instances of molestation and penetrations, I would go into the bathroom and run a tub or sink full of water to make sure that I added plenty of bleach and scrub myself raw. If I did not smell the bleach, then I was not clean. The bathroom would then be dirty because I had washed all the filth off me, so it would have to be cleaned meticulously. Every drain would need to be scrubbed, the floor needed to be mopped, the mirror cleaned the base of the tub scrubbed the entire toilet inside and out and underneath had to be scrubbed, disinfected, and sanitized.

If they accosted me in the area where I slept, then the sheets would have to be washed and the mattress scrubbed to get off any stains flipped over and sprayed down with disinfectant aired out, then the bed remade. The clothes I wore, especially under-garments, had to be washed out by hand and bleached. Then hung to dry and clean clothes had to be put on. This was constant, so when I got older, I kept my home meticulously clean. There was nothing out of place and the smell of bleach had to be in my nostril continuously. It was something that I did not realize was an issue until I had children. My children, just being children, would leave things out of place or dirty items in the sink or a piece of paper on the floor, but that would send me in a complete and total meltdown. I would see the smallest piece of paper as filth, and it would send me into an emotional tailspin. I would start fussing for them to clean up the house and I am sure that my yelling that it was dirty was hurtful to them. When they were smaller, I would constantly pick things up and was always cleaning they had to wash up after every meal. Things had to be always in the proper place there could not be a bottle in the refrigerator out of the place that it was assigned. There could not be any crumbs on the butter, or no condiments could be mixed, no mustard in the mayo jar, no jelly in the peanut butter, no cup out of place, no plate not clean. Because of the trauma and the emotions that came with things being dirty and out of place I was bound by, I took dirt and things out of place as a sign of disrespect. It manifested in ways that were normal to me but abnormal to those around me. It was as if they did not appreciate all the things that I did to keep a roof over their heads and clothes on their back. They were not, in my opinion clean and it hurt me emotionally. I would often be up at one and two in the morning throwing things around cleaning the entire house vacuuming moping dusting cleaning the bathrooms and the whole time crying because it hurt me emotionally that it was not done. There were times this behavior disturbed everyone in the house, and they would get up and just stand around staring often they would say mommy I will clean it up and I would in my state of hurt say it is ok I got it you all don't care how I feel, and it is not clean, to me so I will do it. I did not realize how my words hurt them emotionally until they were older. One day when I was in one of those modes, my youngest asked me. Mommy, what are you cleaning? It isn't dirty and why do you always say that we don't care about you? His question made me stop what I was doing he said, "you always say that we can talk to you about anything, and we can come to you, so I want you to know that it hurts my feelings when you say that I don't care about you or love you because the house isn't clean when I do". The realization hit me that because of the emotional pain that I suffered from and was still bound to in my mind, I was unintentionally inflicting pain on my children, and this was something I vowed I would never do.

Because I was not free from the emotional and traumatic prison of my past, I was inflicting pain on them. It devastated me I went to God in prayer I cried out asking how to fix this. How was I still not over the pain of my past? How was I still messed up from the trauma? How could I do the same thing to my children? I felt like I had caused emotional damage to my children that could never be repaired, that they would hate me for inflicting pain on them. Even my prayer to God was filled with the emotional prison that I lived in. It took God first telling me that my children were not emotionally damaged and traumatized because of me. I went to the extreme and that I needed to calm my spirit. He soothed my troubled heart. He showed me I would never be free and would never grow if I did not turn my emotions over to Him so that He could guide me through them without negative consequences. The way I responded was not normal based on the situation. I would swing to the farthest extreme because what I could control seemed to be out of control. This directly resulted from the emotional trauma I suffered. I could not differentiate the situations from the trauma and it manifested emotionally.

This revelation led me to stay on my face before God for weeks. It also led me to study. I needed to understand freedom from the pain of my past I needed understand how I was still affected by it. This led to me understanding that I never reacted to things how others did. My emotions were off and out of control, and I needed God's help. I needed to be free. I did not want to harm my children. That understanding helped me to see that I needed to be free, and that freedom once achieved led to growth.

Growth is something that we must see to know that He is doing it. That is a negative statement. Growth in God happens when we least expect it. We may not notice it, but someone else may see the growth and that makes the difference. The Bible says that when we accept Jesus into our hearts and into our lives, we become new creatures. Now, while we are growing, we don't grow alone, we grow with the encouragement of God. God wants us to grow in him. In 2 Corinthians 3:17, it states: Now the Lord is that spirit: and where the spirit of the Lord is there is liberty. Well, what does liberty mean? Liberty means the condition of being free, freedom. from this, we understand that in God there is freedom. Freedom to grow by his might and by his power, freedom to come to him and ask whatsoever you will, freedom to serve him in spirit and in truth. Now what does this mean? It means not only is there freedom to grow in God, it means that there is no hindrance. In other words when you turn to the Lord and away from all the pain and hurt of the abuse of the past and your present fear, and problems God will lift the veil that stops us from truly seeing His full Glory, and we can praise and magnify, glorify, and serve him in all Truth.

Now if we then look at the book of Ephesians 4:14-15 (KJV) God tells us we aren't children, that are tossed to and fro and carried about with every wind and doctrine (14a KJV), but speaking the truth in love, my grow up into him in all things, which is the head even Christ (15 KJV). Again, you may ask what this means. It means that when we grow in God; we move from children who can get preoccupied with other things to adults, who can sit and listen to what God is trying to explain to us. It means as adults we understand Christ is the head of our lives, but to understand that we must understand that we must and grow in him. Once we understand God has promised us growth in him, we also understand that he won't just leave us alone to fumble around in the dark. Understand that God has also promised to encourage us along the way. When we examine Psalms 10:17-18 (NIV) It states you hear, O Lord the desire of the afflicted, you encourage them and you listen to their cry, defending the fatherless and the oppressed. In order that man, who is of the earth, may terrify no more. Now that says it all in a nutshell. Growth comes from within through the grace of God. Understand that you will not suddenly stop feeling the pain of your abuse instantly. Some people take years to come to that point, but what we are trying to get you to see is that there is an end to the pain you feel. There is a new sense of oneness from what you have gone through. God wants you to grow to where you can accept his love for you because believe it or not, the actual truth is when your mind is full of painful memories, and you have built a wall around your heart not even God can get in. Why? Because he will not force his way in? He wants you to invite him in, but you must get to the place where you freely let him in.

The following was written shortly after the moments and times I spent with God understanding that I was emotionally bound, and that God was my freedom and in

Him I could grow and learn how to deal with my emotions and be a better parent, pastor, teacher, mentor, and friend to others.

TROUBLE DON'T LAST ALWAYS

There is a pain that is welling up inside of me. I feel as if I am falling apart. My mind races with the things that I need to do. I fear because of the lack of resources I have. There is no way for me to make my financial contributions in this life. I am tired, beaten down, torn, ragged, dejected, oppressed, and sick of the mess. This has got to end. There must be a better way, and there must be something that can be done to make this life more tolerable.

I know the old ones used to say that trouble don't last always, but for me trouble is a way of life. I live in trouble; I wake up in trouble; I go to sleep in trouble; I am ill in trouble, and well in trouble. There is never a moment when trouble is not near me. How do I cope? What do I think? How can I stand? Where is my help? Where is my friend? Where is someone to hold my hand? Where are my good times? Where are my days of peace? Where is my laughter? Where is my rest?

They say that hell is full of people who do wrong and sin against God, but to me, if hell is anything like the life I live, then what is there left for me? I look at my surroundings and I see only despair. I look at my family, the ones who are here, and I look at my life from beginning to this point, and I can't explain the pain that makes me want to die. Inside I feel dejected, inside I feel alone, inside I feel naked, inside I have no home, and each day is like a nightmare, each movement like a sword, each human feeling in me makes me want to run.

So where do I go when this life of mine gets to be too much? I was told to go to the master; at his feet, I will feel his touch. But what is in a touch? I think what can it do for me? Then I think I can handle this life without that kind of thing. But somewhere in my mind and in the pit of all my shame, I begin to realize that this touch could make me whole again, that this touch can take away the pain.

So, I reach for the unknown to touch me, I reach for the hand of someone unseen; I reach for the core of my existence. I reach, I reach, and I reach. And then something happens as I write upon this page; I felt a movement in my heart that is so strange. I have always known pain. This is something I have never heard of. It is something new. What do I do with this feeling? I sit for a moment, and I think of what to do then I feel this different feeling as a light comes shining through, my eyes begin to water, and the tears begin to sting, and I wonder what is going on then it occurs to me. I asked for this touch.

I wanted it so much and now that it is happening, I feel as if I am about to bust. Then he speaks to me through all the haze; he says that I am here, my child. I can take away your pain. I can replace the trouble, I can relieve the shame, and I can make a difference if you just give me your hand. And in that very instant, it becomes so clear to me that God is what I have been longing for and he is all I need.

When I feel lonely and when I feel afraid, I know now that he will comfort me and take away the pain. I understand what I must do, no matter how hard this gets. I must continue to press my way, though. The end is getting closer now and I can see through all the haze. I want to shout for joy this time I can feel something change. I remember a passage of scripture that says I am more than a conqueror.

I remember a song that says I'm pressing my way. I remember those who pray for me each day. I remember there is someone there who will never make me feel ashamed. He will always be my guide, he will never let me fall, he will see me through the trouble and all the bad, he will make something happen in me that will change the way I think, he will give me his peace for that is truly what I seek.

And when the trouble comes again and I feel ready to faint, I have the faith to know he will be there to help me run this race. So, the moral of this story is when you are going through and you feel about crumble, no matter what you do. Look up towards the Master, tell him how you feel, say it any way, you can but only be just real. He wants to hear from you; he is waiting for your call; he is ready to defend you, and he will catch you when you fall.

He will make your life a miracle and bring the light back in, because where the light of Jesus is no darkness can defend, where the love of the Master sits deep within your core will make the devil flee from you and let you worry no more. Stand strong in the knowledge, my friend, that trouble it will come, but understand that through the trouble God will make sure the battle replenishes your soul. Pick up your Bible my child and open up the page drink of the fountain that never runs dry and remember that trouble don't last always.

Questions:

1. Are you emotionally free? Yes or no and why or why not?
2. What do you think you need to do to be free and to grow?

Moment of thought and reflection: Write about how emotional freedom looks to you and how you will achieve it. Analyze how your emotions have dictated how you interact with others and is that interaction harmful to you and them or is it helpful what can you do to improve the way you process and handle emotions.

*keep these notes for your reflection. Talk about them with your circle and support system.

Encouragement to Enlightenment

People who have been through abuse and other types of traumatic events tend to when times are hard to forget that GOD has supplied all our needs. We tend to, as many often do, look at the circumstances and situations that we are dealing with and often lose sight of this. We look at God as elusive and not there as a part of our every-day struggle, forgetting that He is there through it all. The only difference is we forget to tap into the never ending well of strength and comfort that God is and brings to our life daily. God has provided for your needs once don't you think He will do the same for you again. The thing that we forget is that GOD has never stopped encouraging us. He has never stopped guiding and protecting us. He has never stopped being our strength. We just forget that He is there because we have issues looking past our hurt or brokenness to trust that He is there and that He cares.

Since time was time, God has been there for man. Even in the beginning in the garden, God chose to spend time with Adam every day. God would visit Adam in the evening's cool, giving Adam instruction and direction and genuinely spending time with Him. Now, why would God do that? What benefit is it to God to spend time with man? What are His motives and what does He want from us? After all, He is God. What could he possibly want or need from a man? These were questions I asked myself repeatedly over the years and even asked God himself. What do you want from me? Why do you want anything to do with me? Why did you create me?

The answers came to these questions through many different means, first I needed to understand how and why God communicated with man at all. Then I needed to understand why I could not hear him and why I was struggling with all that I went through, even years later, when the trauma and hurt was over. It took me a long time to realize that the pain inflicted from my past was over, but I had not healed from the hurt of it and therefore I was unable to move forward in my life. I was stuck at the point of the initial pain and could not move beyond it. I needed encouragement to accept the things that I experienced to get to an enlightened mindset about the abuse and trauma so that I could move forward. It is essential that you understand I have always had questions about why I had to go through the things that I have and have spent many days and nights on my face asking God these questions. The only thing I wanted to understand was why. I will never fully know and understand the motives of those that perpetrated the hurts and abuse in my life. I just wanted to understand what made me such a target. Not that I would have wanted anyone else to go through the things that I have, but it was a major point of contention for me I did not understand the reason that it was done.

For years I would get hung up on the question, why me? What was it about me that made me such an easy target? Why did I have to be the one who endured this? Why did you abandon me? Why did you let them do this to me? Why did you make me to be a target? Let me help you. I got caught up in the why and as a result, I spent years blocked and lost in the why. I could not get past the why, so I could not get to the breakthrough that I sought so desperately. I thought if God answered the why, then all the pain from the events of trauma in my life would miraculously go away. I was under the presumption that God could and would just wipe those parts of my life from my memory and that I would not have to think about them anymore. That did not happen. Let me encourage you and hopefully it will lead to some enlightenment for you. There will not be a point where everything will be wiped clean, and you will not remember them anymore. That is not how it works. You may always remember the event; however, God will take the pain of that event away if you give it over to Him. Continuing to constantly have the questions why I found kept the pain of the events prevalent in my face and in my life. I realized I gave the memories and hurt the power to continue to control my life. Can I tell you this? It took some time, but I realized that the reason that I could not move forward was fear. That fear gave the memories power. The fear of who I was outside of the things that I endured, the fear that my life was useless or somehow less than because of the abuse, dominated my thoughts. I always felt inadequate and as if my voice did not matter outside of the abuse and trauma. Who was I? Who was I supposed to be? Who would I have been if I had not been a victim of abuse? Where should I go from here? These questions also dominated my thoughts.

Let us look at Psalm 27: 1-3 The Lord is my light and my salvation; whom shall I fear? The Lord is the strength of my life. Of whom shall I be afraid? When the wicked, even mine enemies and my foes came upon me to eat up my flesh they stumbled and fell though an host should encamp against me, my heart shall not fear though war should rise against me, in this will I be confident.

In this scripture, I found a sense of relief and peace. This scripture told me God is not only encouraging me. He is talking about giving me the strength to succeed as well. I must be very honest one thing that made a great impact on my recovery was the fact that at first, I tried to do it alone. I tried to work through the problems that being a survivor of CSA presented in my life without consulting GOD or anyone else for that matter. After giving up on therapy and even for a time giving up on God helping me to deal with the issue, I thought I could do it on my own. This was a mistake. I explored my past in earnest and even sought the help of some unconventional means to figure out where it all went wrong. I wanted to remember everything. I felt that the only way for me to move past it was to remember every little detail every time something happened to me that should not have.

I wanted to have it all out in the open. I wanted my mind to not hold on to the memories. I just wanted to have my mind free. The trickle effect was tiring to me. I was tired of being blindsided by memories that were triggered by different things that I encountered or places I went. I took the time one night and began to really sit and take my time and allow my mind to open and allow memory after memory to flood in. That is when I remembered another incident. For good reason, this was something that I had buried for a long time. This memory was pivotal because it not only took me into one of the worse flashbacks of my life up to that point but also it made me even question the reality of the life I lived. This memory caused me to almost lose my mind. I was not ready to face it alone, and I was definitely not ready for the on slot of emotions and pain that were associated with it, however this memory was the starting point to me saying enough is enough.

Allow me to share a piece with you please be aware this is graphic, and I do not want to cause anyone pain I do however want you to know that sometimes when you have experienced extensive trauma that it may not be such a good idea to seek to the memories and pain from that trauma alone. I know that those who have experienced this type of pain tend to want to go it alone because of the issues that we have with trust but please, please be aware that it is ok to ask for help it is ok to reach out to someone and you do not have to do this alone.

One woman that my dad married said that she thought she was helping me how she saw fit to help me was to severely burn me in my vaginal area. Having someone insert a hot vintage wrought iron hair curler inside of you is a devastating thing to remember, let alone experience. However, she said what she did was to help me. She truly felt at the time or so she said that if she injured me enough, at least then the men who were constantly raping me would have to leave me alone until I healed. I was seven and the pain from that incident still causes me physical issues to this day. Until the moment that this memory surfaced, I simply thought the pain I physically felt during intercourse resulted from the many incidences of rape and forced penetration that I experienced as a child. My mind blocked the incident because it was so traumatic. When that memory came back to me, I almost lost my mind. Not just the image came back, but the pain of the incident came back as well. My mind could not control what I was feeling, and for me, control was very important. I was alone. The memory overtook me. The pain overwhelmed me and for a long period I lay on the floor of my closet crying out in agony and shame. After regaining composure, and the pain subsided, I realized I should not have tried to deal with the issues of my past on my own. I also realized that I needed someone or something stronger than myself to help me through this.

This memory caused me to go into a very serious depression, so I am telling you this is not something that I recommend you try to handle by yourself. You must have a support system to tackle these issues. You must have someone to lean on when these types of memories surface. As much as I prefer my solitude, I had to learn that I could not possibly do this alone. For me, I needed God, the only constant in my life, the only thing stronger than the memories and pain. The only being that was strong enough for me to lean on. At the time, there was no one and nothing there to comfort me (or so I felt). Because I separated myself from every other person in my world. I did not know how to lean on them or trust them with my truth, so I shut everyone out.

After this moment, I went back to my source of strength, which was and always will be God. I poured myself into the other love that I have in my life, writing in doing so God moved me to write the following: This poem encouraged me and gave me strength long after I had written it. This poem was my way of expressing the strength of the Lord in my life and the encouragement that he gave me to take the steps forward in order not to just help myself but to help you as well. I want you to understand that my focus is to help you get through all the bitterness of your abuse and to move to a place of acceptance of the abuse and eventually to a point of forgiveness of the person who abused you and to forgive yourself. As I share another piece of my heart with you, I pray it ministers to your soul and encourages you to know you will make it despite what you feel now and what it looks like. The dream that you have for complete peace and freedom in your mind and life is attainable. You are Victorious and you are walking in victory even though right now you may not feel like it or see it. However, I pray that something in this book will help you realize that dream.

Realizing A Dream

Within her soul a dam breaks her tears coat her face like the rain coats the forest floor. Her heart is filled with a sense of need and longing. She senses within herself that the time has come in her life when she must choose the path that she will travel. Should she choose the path that is wide and open to all creatures of sin and degradation, or should she choose the straight and narrow path that leads to righteousness and peace of mind?

She waits on the brink of an abyss so full that her soul threatens to float away in the darkness; she continues to cry; the tears running down on her cheeks like tracks forged from a river. Then suddenly she realizes at that moment which path she must choose. She knows she must choose the narrow path, for it is the path that will set her free.

She takes a step, then falters for just a fleeting moment. She rethinks her decision and then, in a flash, it is gone she steps forward again. The force of her thoughts makes her falter once more is she really doing the right thing is she really making the right decision is there some other way to fulfill her obligation, she takes a deep breath the air that fills her lungs is tainted with the stench of cowardice and fear. It angers her that she is so weak and lost in her our thoughts that she cannot take the step that she needs to finish what was begun so many years ago.

She closes her eyes and holds out her hands, then she does it. She finally does it she leaps from the mountain that she has been stranded on for so long and plummets into the abyss. Into the pain and torment, into the bitterness. At first, it seems as if she has made a mistake. The pain that comes is so great it shatters her will, like a glass falling to the floor.

Her eyes feel as if they are being scratched out by eagles. She feels a deep sense of remorse and dread. Then it happens she feels as if she is floating and something no someone is carrying her to safety, someone is holding her safe and warm. The feeling of relief washes over her. She senses a peace that is more real than the pain she felt moments before. She realizes that her feet have touched the ground. She stopped and looks then listens. There is a sound inaudible at first, then it becomes clear, a whisper in the air, a faint voice that sounds like the gentle whistle of the trees. She strains to hear. She wants desperately to understand the voice she hears. She wants to see who the voice belongs to; she waits and listens. Then it becomes clear that she is not alone, and she feels fear once more, but the voice speaks softly and sweetly in her ear.

It says I am here. I have always been here. I am He who sent thee to do my will. It is I who carried you through the pain it is I who dried your cheeks from the tears that stained them; it is I who have supplied all of your needs and it is I who will walk with you, even carry you through the times to come. She feels peace like a river in the middle of a forest peace that seeps into her soul and fills her damaged heart with love peace that starts to remove the pain. She reaches out and touches His hand. She feels the warmth that fills her soul she holds on and weeps.

He stands there and lets her weep for only a few moments, then He dries her tears. And into her heart he places a word and says tell it everywhere you go, tell the world that I am he who will be there when you need me the most. Tell them I am the one who watches them as they sleep. Tell them I am to one who lives within their hearts and knows all their hopes and fears. Tell them I am the way the truth and the light. She holds on tighter, for she has finally understood the years of pain and anguish. She finally realizes her purpose. She bows low and says, Lord, take not only my hand but take also my heart. Do with me and through me what you will. I give myself to you to be used as an instrument of love and peace.

Then she says thank you Lord for all the times you carried me in the past and for all the times you will carry me in the future. She places her soul in his hand and there he holds it, protected from the horror of this life. There he keeps her safe from all harm there is where she will stay forever endeavoring to do his will.

I want to encourage you because I have no desire for it to take you the years that it took me to find peace. I want you to find peace, move forward with your life, and live it to the fullest. I have a great desire to see all who have been affected by abuse and trauma happy, whole, healthy, and free. I want no one to feel what I have over the years. I want you to know that this may be difficult, and you may want to give in sometimes, but hold on. This book is intended to be a starting point in your life and a way for you to know and understand that you are not alone and that there are others who are here to support you as you begin your journey to peace and happiness and wholeness.

Questions:

1. *Do you feel as though you will move to a place of peace about your past?*
2. *Why are you afraid? When did this fear set in?*

3. *Do you feel as though you will be in this place forever? Are you strong enough to do this or do you feel as though you may need assistance?*
4. *Would you be willing to join or start a support group to help others as well as continue your journey to overcoming the abuse you suffered?*
5. *Do you feel you suffer more than others? Did you feel as though you were targeted to be abused?*
6. *Do you still blame yourself for the abuse? Do you still hold bitterness in your heart towards your abuser or abusers?*
7. *Do you doubt God or yourself? If God, why? If yourself Why?*

You've made it this far. What now?

Finally, you made it to the last of this book, but not the end of your journey. I hope that you have been encouraged and learned some things about your struggle and how you feel about yourself. Now the genuine work begins. I wanted to leave you on a note of encouragement and true understanding. I have said throughout this entire book I could not do this without God. No, I am saying you must have to serve God. I am telling you that for me, I could not do this without Him. God has been there from the beginning and yes, even though I have been angry with Him for things that I felt He did not save me from. I would not give up my relationship with Him for anything in the world. God has always been my help and hope and my peace. Even amid the most difficult times that you have ahead, I need you to grab hold of your relationship with God with all that you have.

Let me say this: I have tried to deal with the hurt of my life by myself, in therapy, with medication, and without. I have tried ignoring it, letting it take over every aspect of my life. I have fallen into depression, had anxiety attacks, suffered flashbacks, experienced CPTSD.

Suffered with addiction form everything from cigarettes to cocaine, and prescription drugs from the time I was 14 until my late twenties trying to deal with all the pain and hurt from growing up in an abusive environment and living in an abusive environment for almost 27 years. I know I would not have made it without God. Why? Because God is my refuge.

What do I mean by God is my refuge look with me at Psalm 46: 1, 7 (KJV) God is our refuge and, strength, a very present help in trouble. The Lord of hosts is with us. The God of Jacob is our refuge. Selah. Refuge, according to Webster's New World Dictionary and Thesaurus, is a shelter or protection from danger, difficulty, a place of protection, shelter, sanctuary, retreat, hiding place, haven, fortress, and stronghold.

I know you may say, but I still got hurt, or I still got raped, or I still got molested, or my spouse still beats me. Why doesn't God stop them? Or you may say, so how or why do you still say that God is your refuge after all that you went through? Why do you still trust Him? My answer: No matter where I go in this life or what I do, there has been only one constant in my life. Even when I wanted nothing to do with Him and walked away from Him out of anger, bitterness, depression, and fear, He was still there. When I turned away and refused to do anything associated with or related to Him, God was still there. He knew I was hurt; He knew I was broken; He knew I was bound, and He was still there. All God has ever wanted was for me to be free and all He wants is to take your pain away and for you to be free and happy and whole.

Before I give you my final thoughts and last bits of what I hope has been some sense of encouragement. I need to be clear. My foundation and belief are in God and no matter where I am in this Journey it always will be. For me, there are some absolutes in this life and one of them is God that is the foundation of my world, and I am glad that it is and would not have it any other way. I started this book out by saying that if that is not the belief that you have and that you do not have a relationship with God, then you should establish one. I will say again I did not say immediately to find a church, doctrine, dogma, theology, or religion. Establish a relationship with God. He will direct you to the rest. I did not say that this was going to be easy. I did not say that you are going to spend the rest of your life with overjoyed days and blissful nights. In fact, the first part of this journey is going to be rough, and it is going to take a lot out of you. I implore you to seek a relationship with the Master and let Him help you through this. If that is too difficult for you to do for various reasons, do not think that you will never get help, or you are stuck. That is not the way the God I serve operates. Because I believe in Him, and I believe He gave me this work to do, and I believe that by working through this book and being a part of or establishing a circle of people who have been through this as well, you will be healed. I declare you will be delivered and set free from the pain that the abuse has caused you. I know God will give harmony to your heart and ease to your mind. God will give you rest and help you on your journey. I know God will never leave you alone and will send those He chooses to help you on this journey. When you want to give up and throw in the towel, I speak rejuvenation to your mind and determination to your heart with a fresh wind to help you push through. While you are going through fighting the thought of wanting to be free and fear of what that really means, I know God will bring peace and relief to your heart. I know God will do all these things for you and more.

Why do I believe this so strongly? Because I asked God to do it for you. I asked God to help you get to a place of peace, happiness, and wholeness just as He has guided me. I asked Him to do for you what He has done for me, and I know He is going to do it. He will not leave you broken and alone, and I have enough faith in him to know that. That is the difference between religion and relationship. When you have a relationship with God, you have an innate trust in everything that you place in His hands, and you believe all that He is and does is only to help you, not to hurt you. Having a relationship with God is a hard concept for those who have brokenness, but you can. He awaits you with open arms. He doesn't want to hurt you He only wants you whole.

What being in a broken state meant to me early in my life was that I could not connect with people how I should have. Some of this can be supported by clinical science about the effects of trauma during early development. I do not want to discuss that from a clinical point of view I want to talk to you about it from a personal point of view and maybe my experience will help you understand even more that you are not in this alone.

Being in a place of brokenness takes a toll on the mind but also on the body as well. Above all else, in my opinion, it takes a toll on the soul. That inner most part of you, the person you cannot and do not bear to anyone, especially when you have been hurt. For me, I was so isolated from people because I found that was the easiest way to protect myself. If I never let you close to me, then you could not hurt me.

Early in this process, when it became apparent, I was going to need someone to help me deal with the residual effects of the abuse. I tried to find at least one person who I could confide in. At first it was my mother, but she only used the things that I said when I was feeling my worse to later throw them back in my face when we would argue. Resulting in even more hurt. I tried therapist and found that because of the extent of the abuse, some could not handle the depth of the pain that was a prevailing thought in my mind. I found they felt the only course of action was heavy psychological medication that kept me feeling like I was not myself. Or I have had a therapist say to me they are just not equipped to handle my type of case. Therapy and counseling have changed drastically since I first tried therapy over 20 years ago, and they are more advanced. I turned to my pastors who in turn just told me that if I had enough faith, I would not still be dealing with the issues I was and I needed to fast and pray more. Because it seemed to me like there was never a human that I could turn to, I poured all that was in my heart out to God. I did not realize at the time that my soul was fractured seriously fractured. Not only was I broken mentally, but my soul was broken physically. The pain of being repeatedly abused over the years had impacted me so profoundly spiritually that my soul hurt and longed for peace.

So not only was I dealing with thoughts of suicide because mentally I could not take the pain at the height of the worst part of this journey for me in what seemed like the perfect storm, my soul gave up as well. There was a series of events and weeks of major depression that led up to that last suicide attempt that early evening in September 2004, after an extensive knockdown drag out argument with my mother, rejection from a manipulative pastor, attacked by my mother's lover, a diagnosis from the doctor that was devastating and my own mental battle of guilt, shame, and worthlessness my heart and my soul fell into alignment, and I was done.

That night I felt that the last piece of my soul that kept me here, kept me sane, kept me seeking answers from God gave up. I now know that it was truly a trick of the enemy using all the elements of my life to converge in what seemed like the most unbearable overwhelming situation one could ever be in, but at that moment, that was not what I felt. I felt disconnected from my source of strength, disjointed from the thing that gave me peace and solace. It was as if my soul, that part of me that is the deepest depths of my existence, the thing that makes me who I am just gave in to the years of pain and hurt. There was not one person who at that moment would have been able to stop the mental and emotional storm that lead up to that moment and had I not felt so completely utterly shattered and alone I do not think that I would have attempted to take my own life, however because I did not trust people I had no one that I could reach out to and again felt like I just couldn't take it anymore. In that moment, I felt abandoned, even by God. It has taken some time and evaluation about that night what I can remember for me to piece one thing together even though I felt alone. I wasn't. God was there.

I know you are asking, but what about God being your refuge? If He wasn't there for you then when you needed Him most, then why do you still lean on Him? why is He your refuge?

The answer is straightforward, because if it had not been for God that night, I would not be here. It was God who stopped me from taking every bottle of pills in the house; it was God who allowed my brother in the Gospel to call that night. God troubled his spirit and let him know there was something wrong. It was God who moved the police to protect me from my mother when she came back to argue more, even after finding out that I swallowed an unknown quantity of pills. It was God who led the doctor and the nurses who treated me and God that kept me in my right mind after swallowing so many pills that they could only recover a few hundred. I lean on Him because even when I really didn't feel Him; he was still there, still my protector, still my doctor and my guide. Still the heartbeat of my life and still the keeper of my soul. No matter how far I have strayed and how much I have questioned Him. He has never left me or forsaken me. I couldn't feel Him because I was broken and my understanding of Him was limited. As I sought a genuine relationship with Him and my trust in Him grew, so did my understanding of how much He was there for me.

The concept of religion differs from the understanding of God. Religion is a set of beliefs and doctrines that have been taught or handed down. Something that we do sometimes even without thinking. It is a way for man to take the responsibility of the atrocities of life off of themselves and put them on something else: God. This way, man does not have to take accountability for their own shortcomings. When you develop a relationship with God, you understand you are entering a mutually exclusive situation with your creator and, much like a human relationship as your trust in Him grows, so does your understanding of who he is.

I want you all to take the time and find something besides yourself to depend and rely on. Find someone besides you to walk this journey out with. Find a place or create a safe space for not only yourself but for others whom you know who have suffered and walk this thing out together. This book was not written from the model of walking this out alone it was written in the format that would cause you to look within yourself to answer the questions and to find or start a support group compiled of others who have gone through what you have and need someone to confide in. This book is the beginning of the circle as you find, others add them to the circle embrace them, help them, confide in them, and let them confide in you. Start small and stay close to each other. Hold each other up. You may have walked this alone before now, but you no longer have to.

Walk this out with someone and remember, I am not planning on leaving you all alone to deal with the memories and issues that even reading this book may have caused. I plan to be there. I am the beginning of your circle. I am praying for you and with you. I want to be that compass in the storm that points true north and, with God, I will continue to pray and intercede on your behalf. Even if your faith and relationship is not strong enough or at this time, you do not believe in Him at all I do and because of the Faith I have in Him, He has given me the strength to be there for you. I am here because when I was at my lowest; I had no one and I won't let that happen to someone else. I refuse to be like those in ministry who could not or would not help me get through this. I am determined to devote my time and resources to helping those who have gone through hurt, brokenness, and abuse. You will not be alone. There are people designed and sent by God to assist you. Even you who have taken the time to read this book you are now a resource for someone else. You can be the first leg in the circle if you feel this book has helped you and you know of someone who has been through the same or similar situations. When you finish reading this book, take the first step. Send this book to someone who is hurting or broken. If you are ready, give them a glimpse into why you sent this book to them. Then prepare to step in and be a support for them. You begin to build your circle let them know you are there for them. Support them like you wanted and still need to be supported. If you feel led start in your area a support group, go through this book discuss the questions. Build an infrastructure around each other and be there for one another as I am here for you and as God is always there with you and for you.

It takes you being willing to come out of your protective bubble and speak up. You need to continue to seek resources and guidance from every probable source that can help you and if you cannot find a resource, do what I was led to: create one. This Journey for me will never be over but I can walk the rest of the way knowing that not only did I survive and overcome abuse with God at the forefront but that because I survived and overcame, it was and is my honor to give this work to the world so that it may help someone to finally live not just exist but to truly live a whole and healed life. Remember, It is all in the Journey and exercise in Faith.

A letter Of Completion from the desk of the author

Greetings,

It is with Great pleasure I greet you again now that you have completed this book. I pray that something within these pages has helped you to move with God to another level in your life. You are now a part of the Journey Family. We are more than happy to continue to pray with you and for you as you walk away from your past, move out of abusive situations, enjoy your presence, and look forward to your future. I am going to ask you to now take a leap of Faith, share this book with someone, reach out and connect with others who have gone through the same situations as you have. Support them, help them get through the pain of their abuse. There are resources at the back of this book that you can refer to also join us on the It's All in the Journey Facebook page. There, you will find inspirational messages and words of encouragement. Other resources are on the way. Look out for the It's All in the Journey Website and the Journey Family podcast. We look forward to helping those who would like to connect directly by offering to be a listening ear. Helping other organizations or churches set up support groups to go through the material in this book and consulting with those organizations and others to start support groups for those who have been abused in their regions. We want to build a community of people with one purpose: helping each other heal from the hurt that abuse has caused.

God Bless you.

Apostle Lesa Hunt

Will you accept the assignment?

I pray that through reading this material that you have understood that God love you and that he wants the best for you; I have truly enjoyed my journey so far since the day that I took the chance to trust God in this process. Know that you are loved, you are special; you are important. You have endured unspeakable devastation because of circumstances that were thrust upon you by others, and you survived. Now I hope to help you get some footing and foundation so that you can overcome them with the guidance of The Father in a genuine relationship with Him. Not a religious ideology, not a doctrine, not a dogma, but a real genuine relationship. You have God you always have and now you have me and the rest of the Journey Family. This issue is so close to my heart that I cannot wait to see you grow, change, become more confident, and blossom again. I want you to live your life and let your light shine. Never hide it again under a bush or rock. Never let another person steal your joy or your peace. You are force in the earth a power to not be taken lightly. You are strong; you are brave; you are unique in your experience and your way of thinking. You are perfect to God; He loves you no matter what other think or say and all he wants is a relationship with you and the opportunity to heal the hurts and wounds of your life. Give Him that opportunity the chance to have an authentic, intimate, one-on-one relationship with you. Let Him in to comfort you during the difficult times and bring you peace and joy like never before.

Now, if while you were reading this book, you felt the urge or desire to share this with someone else who has gone through similar experiences. If you feel like I felt and just want someone to know that they are not alone. They do not have to feel like you felt stuck, hurt, broken, bitter, angry, guilty, and full of shame. Then I want to challenge you, if you know someone who could benefit from this book and benefit from having a community of people who will be there to support them and help them through the rough road ahead. Start the circle with you. Start by sending them this book, but before you do, share with them why you feel this book may help them. Be the first foundation of a support group for each other. Let them know what helped you with this material and be there to be a listening ear for them. Give to someone else what was given to you a chance to change the way they view themselves and the beginning of the healing that, like you, they so desperately need. Take a moment write out how you felt when you started this Journey and where you are now that you have finished the book. Add where you would like to be in your life if you have not yet achieved all that you would like to accomplish. If you are interested in starting a support network for others, then take the time to write out a plan. Reach out to It's all in the Journey on Facebook and we will work together to help you. I look forward to seeing you on your Journey to happiness and wholeness. Stay well and stay Blessed keep fighting. You are destined to WIN!!

Scriptures to meditate on: Taken from the King James Version, New Living Translation, New International Version. Take the time to meditate on these scriptures and find others on your own as your relationship with God grows, so will your base of Scriptures. These scriptures are scriptures of hope, healing, and seeking God.

1Peter 5:7 Casting all your cares upon him for He careth for you. (KJV)

Isaiah 41:10 Fear thou not; for I am with thee: be not dismayed; for I am thy God: I will strengthen thee; yea, I will help thee; yea, I will uphold thee with the right hand of my righteousness. (KJV)

Jeremiah 29:11 For I know the thoughts that I think toward you, saith the LORD, thoughts of peace, and not of evil, to give you an expected end. (KJV)

Psalms 9:9 The Lord is a shelter for the oppressed, a refuge in times of trouble. (NLT)

Psalms 9:10 Those who know your name trust in you, for you, O Lord, do not abandon those who search for you. (NLT)

Psalms 91:2 This I declare about the Lord: He alone is my refuge, my place of safety; he is my God, and I trust him. (NLT)

Matthew 11:28 Then Jesus said, "Come to me, all of you who are weary and carry heavy burdens, and I will give you rest. (NLT)

Romans 15:13. "May the God of hope fill you with all joy and peace as you trust in him, so that you may overflow with hope by the power of the Holy Spirit." (NIV)

Psalm 30:2 the psalmist says, "LORD my God, I called to you for help, and you healed me." (NIV)

Acts 17:27 That they should seek the Lord, if haply they might feel after him, and find him, though he be not far from every one of us (KJV)

2 Chronicles 7:14 If my people, which are called by my name, shall humble themselves, and pray, and seek my face, and turn from their wicked ways; then will I hear from heaven, and will forgive their sin, and will heal their land. (KJV)

Acts 17:27-28 That they should seek the Lord, if haply they might feel after him, and find him, though he be not far from every one of us: For in him we live, and move, and have our being; as certain also of your own poets have said, For we are also his offspring. (KJV)

Jeremiah 30:17 For I will restore health unto thee, and I will heal thee of thy wounds, saith the Lord; because they called thee an Outcast, saying, This is Zion, whom no man seeketh after.(KJV)

Jeremiah 33:6 Behold, I will bring it health and cure, and I will cure them, and will reveal unto them the abundance of peace and truth.(KJV)

Psalm 107:19-21 Then they cry unto the Lord in their trouble, and he saveth them out of their distresses. He sent his word, and healed them, and delivered them from their destructions. Oh that men would praise the Lord for his goodness, and for his wonderful works to the children of men!(KJV)

Isaiah 53:4-5 Surely he hath borne our griefs, and carried our sorrows: yet we did esteem him stricken, smitten of God, and afflicted. But he was wounded for our transgressions, he was bruised for our iniquities: the chastisement of our peace was upon him; and with his stripes we are healed.(KJV)

Citations:

Koenig H. G. (2012). Religious versus Conventional Psychotherapy for Major Depression in Patients with Chronic Medical Illness: Rationale, Methods, and Preliminary Results. *Depression research and* treatment, 2012, 460419. https://doi.org/10.1155/2012/460419

Palic, S., Zerach, G., Shevlin, M., Zeligman, Z., Elklit, A., & Solomon, Z. (2016). Evidence of complex posttraumatic stress disorder (CPTSD) across populations with prolonged trauma of varying interpersonal intensity and ages of exposure. Psychiatry research, 246, 692–699. 13https://doi.org/10.1016/j.psychres.2016.10.062

De Jongh, A., Resick, P. A., Zoellner, L. A., van Minnen, A., Lee, C. W., Monson, C. M., Foa, E. B., Wheeler, K., Broeke, E. T., Feeny, N., Rauch, S. A., Chard, K. M., Mueser, K. T., Sloan, D. M., van der Gaag, M., Rothbaum, B. O., Neuner, F., de Roos, C., Hehenkamp, L. M., Rosner, R., ... Bicanic, I. A. (2016). CRITICAL ANALYSIS OF THE CURRENT TREATMENT GUIDELINES FOR COMPLEX PTSD IN ADULTS. Depression and anxiety, 33 (5), 359–369. https://doi.org/10.1002/da.22469

Bierman A. The Effects of Childhood Maltreatment on Adult Religiosity and Spirituality: Rejecting God the Father Because of Abusive Fathers? *J. Sci. Study Relig.* 2005; 44:349–359. Doi: 10.1111/j.1468-5906.2005.00290.x. [CrossRef] [Google Scholar] [Ref list]

How children cope with ongoing threat and trauma: The BASIC Ph Model, Frank

Zenere, EdS, Crisis Management Specialist for Miami-Dade Public Schools and a former member of NASP's National Emergency Assistance Team. www.nasponline.org

The Holy Bible: King James Version. (2011). Hendrickson. (Original work published 1611)

Holy Bible: New Living Translation. 2015. Carol Stream, IL: Tyndale House Publishers

New International Version Bible. (2011). Zondervan. (Original work published 1978)

Apostle Lesa Hunt is the Presiding Prelate and Founder of Restored for His Glory International Fellowship Inc. The Leader of New Restoration Divine Deliverance International Ministries, Inc. and she is the President and Founder of Complete Restoration Publishing, LLC. Apostle Lesa is the Author if It's All in the Journey an Exercise in Faith. Apostle Lesa's personal experiences with surviving childhood CSA and trauma and years of working with those affected by molestation, rape, and abuse fuels her desire to help those living with the results of such abuse. Apostle Lesa Hunt has spent years taking courses and receiving training in Clinical Mental Health Counseling, Pastoral Counseling and Pursuing her advanced degree in Mental Health Counseling. Apostle Lesa spends her time helping others and raising her two younger sons. She loves to take a moment at the beach spending time with God by the water, allowing the cares of this life to melt away. Apostle Lesa's one desire is to help those who feel broken and bound by the pain of their past recover all and live a happy, healthy, prosperous life.